Beyond the Pitch

Beyond the Pitch

The Founder's Guide to Navigating Capital, Investors, and Growth Without Losing Control

Avery Stanton

Mindful Pages

Published in 2025

ISBN: 9789371770477 (PB)
ISBN: 9789371777421 (eBook)

Published by

Mindful Pages
Imprint of Alpha Editions LLC
312 W. 2nd St #1834
Casper, WY 82601, USA

This book was developed using advanced writing tools to support the drafting and ideation process. All content has been thoughtfully curated, refined, and reviewed to ensure quality and relevance.

Content

Introduction
The Real Game Starts After the Money Lands

There is a persistent illusion that haunts many founders: the belief that securing an investor's "yes" marks the pinnacle of the journey. For countless entrepreneurs, that moment—when the term sheet is signed, the funds arrive, and the press release circulates—feels like ultimate vindication. Years of bootstrapping, convincing sceptical customers, and pitching to indifferent investors suddenly yield applause. Friends congratulate you, headlines hail you as "one to watch," and your team dreams aloud about the projects now within reach. Champagne is poured, and for a fleeting instant, it seems the hardest part is behind you.

It is not.

If you have navigated the early chaos of a startup and successfully attracted external capital, you have not reached the summit—you have arrived at base camp. Ahead lies the steepest, most precarious stretch of the ascent. The air is thinner here; errors are magnified. Every decision is scrutinised more intensely, the stakes higher, and the terrain far less forgiving. Moreover, the higher you climb, the more stakeholders—financial, strategic, and emotional—are invested in each move.

The first truth to accept is this: raising capital is not the conclusion of the founder's challenge; it is the onset of a fundamentally different one. From the moment the wire transfer clears, your role transforms. No longer merely a scrappy entrepreneur navigating by instinct and adrenaline, you become a custodian of other people's money—a steward of capital, trust, and expectations. New stakeholders arrive on the scene: investors with their own agendas, timetables, and influence over your decisions. Whether actively on your board or quietly observing from the cap table, their presence reshapes the gravitational pull of your company's choices.

This shift—subtle at first, then unmistakable—requires more than operational adjustments; it demands a recalibration of identity. The qualities that made you effective before funding do not automatically sustain you after. Scrappiness can appear reckless, the impulse to seize every opportunity may be read as undisciplined, and autonomy becomes shared governance. Every bold move must now be weighed against burn rate, strategic milestones, and investor confidence.

Herein lies the paradox: the very capital you laboured to secure can become both your greatest asset and your most dangerous liability. Abundance tempts. You hire faster than culture can assimilate. You pursue markets that distract from core advantages. You build infrastructure for a future not yet guaranteed. In the glow of fresh funding, momentum can easily masquerade as inevitability.

This book exists to interrupt that pattern—to show that post-funding leadership is a distinct discipline, with its own principles, pitfalls, and practices. We will not dwell on crafting the perfect pitch deck or negotiating valuation; others have covered "getting to yes." Our concern begins where that journey ends: the moment the real work starts, when the rules have changed and the stakes rise.

The pressures following a funding round are nothing new, yet in today's venture environment, they are amplified. Speed is often mistaken for progress. Investors expect rapid scaling not because it is always wise, but because the model rewards narratives of swift dominance. Founders are subtly—and sometimes overtly—pushed to spend faster, chase larger valuations, and act with relentless urgency. Those who resist can be branded as unambitious; those who comply without discipline risk burning their advantage before it solidifies.

Mismanaging this phase is unforgiving. Companies falter not necessarily due to product failure but from leadership losing control of pace, focus, or stakeholder alignment. Founders are replaced not for lack of vision but for failing to adapt to new governance realities. Teams splinter, culture erodes, and what once felt like an unstoppable ascent ends in an unceremonious descent—often without the founder on board.

Conversely, founders who master this environment can transform capital into a force multiplier. They leverage investor relationships strategically, treat milestones as negotiation tools, build infrastructure that scales reliably, and exercise constraint as deliberately as they pursue growth. Most importantly, they preserve the clarity of purpose that brought them to this point—something no balance sheet can buy.

Throughout these chapters, you will learn to treat capital not as a cushion but as a catalyst—something to be managed with precision. You will discover how investor relationships evolve after the deal closes, how to maintain influence without surrendering control, and why a thoughtful capital deployment plan is a strategic instrument rather than a mere financial exercise. Milestones will be shown as levers of operational progress and instruments of political positioning.

We will confront the harder truths: scaling too quickly can hollow out culture, "no" can be the most strategic word, and effective board management often begins long before the meeting convenes. The psychological demands of post-funding leadership—the isolation, stress, and temptation to equate worth solely with valuation—will also be explored, along with practical methods to preserve resilience.

Crucially, we will maintain a long-term perspective. Funding rounds are chapters, not conclusions. Success is measured not by the capital raised but by whether the company becomes resilient, adaptable, and ultimately self-sustaining. Whether your goal is exit or continued growth, your greatest leverage comes from controlling your destiny rather than relying on the next round to rescue it.

Post-funding leadership deserves recognition as a distinct discipline, defined by unique principles and methods. It combines strategic finance, investor diplomacy, operational foresight, and cultural stewardship. It is not merely "running a company with more money"—it is operating under new physics, where the mass of capital changes the trajectory of every decision.

This book offers frameworks and tools to navigate that terrain with clarity, confidence, and control. You will find strategic lenses for decision-making, practical approaches to managing investor relations, and behavioural insights to thrive under relentless pressure.

The investor's "yes" is not the final step. It is the beginning of a more complex, high-stakes phase—one that can elevate you to extraordinary achievements or overwhelm you entirely. By recognising the reality, preparing deliberately, and acting with discipline, you can not only survive this stage—you can master it.

Welcome to base camp. The climb starts here.

Chapter 1
The Post-Funding Identity Shift

It is hard to exaggerate the intensity of that first post-funding moment. For months, perhaps years, you have been navigating a near-constant state of tension—scraping together dwindling reserves, negotiating extended supplier credit, persuading early hires to accept equity in lieu of cash, and convincing yourself that sheer grit can substitute for resources. Then, almost imperceptibly, the landscape shifts. The wire transfer clears. The pressure of survival seems, at least superficially, to ease. Yet if the pre-funding phase is defined by an outward struggle for capital, the post-funding phase demands an inward one: a psychological recalibration from hustler to steward, from improviser to strategist.

This is not merely a matter of scale; it is a question of identity. Before funding, authority rested on the immediacy of vision and a willingness to assume risk. Decisions were yours alone, advice optional, and control absolute. After funding, the ground beneath you moves. You answer not only to your team and customers but also to those who have invested millions in your ability to generate value, often under conditions and timelines not of your choosing. The weight of that responsibility is invisible to anyone who has not borne it. Capital does more than finance the next chapter of your company—it rewrites who holds the pen.

From this point forward, every decision carries a dual charge: operational consequences for your business and political consequences for investor relationships. You are now managing two markets simultaneously: the tangible market for your product and the financial market that exists inside your boardroom. This duality is where many founders stumble. The instincts that once ensured survival—reactive decisions, opportunistic spending, gut-led pivots—can become liabilities if applied without recognising that the rules have fundamentally changed.

This recalibration is not a discretionary leadership upgrade; it is a mechanism of survival. Even the most promising venture can unravel without it. Consider the founder flush with Series A funds who expands into multiple regions within months, only to find operational complexity has outpaced managerial bandwidth. Or the founder accustomed to unilateral decision-making who alienates a board expecting deliberation and data-backed insights. In both cases, the setback arises not from market forces but from a disconnect between pre-funding mindset and post-funding reality.

Understanding this transition begins with recognising the new power dynamics. Pre-funding, the investor is a potential ally whose approval you seek. Post-funding, they become a continuous stakeholder whose influence permeates every decision. Early signs may appear subtle: requests for more granular metrics, invitations to consider initiatives you had not prioritised. Gradually, the asymmetry becomes apparent—leadership remains yours, but authority is shared. The vote is no longer solely yours to cast.

Communication must evolve alongside this shift. Investors are not passive recipients; they interpret updates through their strategic lenses. A measured delay in product launch may read as loss of momentum. Frugality might appear as a lack of ambition. Every board presentation, email, or casual update becomes an instrument of influence, recalibrating confidence and shaping future support.

The transition from autonomy to accountability is often jarring. Decisiveness, once a hallmark of leadership, now exists alongside consultation and consensus-building. Input must be solicited, stakeholders aligned, rationale documented—a process that can feel bureaucratic. Yet, when navigated skillfully, this discipline enhances authority. Accountability is not surrender; it is the exercise of power with foresight and transparency. Founders who embrace it learn to convert perceived constraints into leverage, using the board's collective insight to sharpen strategy and buffer against unforeseen shocks.

There is, however, an uncomfortable truth: this shift is as emotional as it is structural. For many, the company embodies selfhood. External capital can feel like shared ownership of that identity. Decisions are no longer exclusively yours, and with that comes a sense of intrusion. Natural reactions emerge: subtle resistance, withholding information, executing initiatives without discussion, framing updates to pre-empt scrutiny. Such tactics may preserve a fleeting sense of independence but erode trust and jeopardise long-term investor relationships.

Real-world examples illustrate both the risk and reward of adaptation. A health-tech founder, following a significant Series B, acknowledged her limitations in regulatory management. Rather than cling to operational control, she appointed a seasoned COO, refocused on vision and partnerships, and doubled the company's valuation in eighteen months. Contrast this with a consumer-app founder who insisted on total creative control, disregarding investor concerns about unsustainable marketing spend. Within a year, escalating acquisition costs and declining engagement forced a dilutive down round, stripping him of majority control.

These are not tales of morality but of adaptation. Thriving post-funding is less about surrender and more about expansion—integrating the urgency and flexibility of the scrappy founder with the foresight and discipline of a capital steward. It demands fluency in two languages: the improvisational, creative idiom of entrepreneurship and the measured, evidence-driven discourse of governance.

This chapter will dissect each facet of the post-funding identity shift. We will explore why moving from survivalist to steward is a change in operating system, not merely job description. We will examine navigating new power structures without losing strategic agency, translating accountability into influence, and spotting early warning signs of the "scale-up shock" that can destabilise even well-funded ventures. By the end, you will understand the mechanics of this transformation and how to approach it deliberately, safeguarding both company trajectory and your capacity to lead.

In the post-funding world, the question ceases to be whether you can secure capital—it becomes whether you can grow into the leader capable of knowing what to do with it.

From Scrappy Founder to Capital Steward

The transition from running a start-up on fumes to managing millions in investor capital is not merely a change in resources; it is a profound shift in identity, one that many founders underestimate until they are in the midst of it. What was once a personal crusade powered by ingenuity and relentless willpower becomes a shared enterprise subject to external expectations, formal oversight, and new measures of success. The founder who once made decisions at kitchen tables, fuelled by instinct and a sense of urgency, must now operate in a world where every choice is weighed against its implications for valuation, runway, and investor confidence. This is not a matter of learning new skills alone—it is a psychological metamorphosis, and without deliberate recalibration, it is dangerously easy to self-sabotage.

In the scrappy phase, survival sharpens the senses. Every hire is a bet you cannot afford to lose, every customer win is a lifeline, and every expenditure is considered with the gravity of a personal risk. Decisions are immediate, unencumbered by the need for formal consensus. That urgency, though exhausting, carries its own clarity. You are the arbiter of direction, the custodian of vision, and the chief executor of strategy. When you succeed, it is because you willed it so; when you fail, there is no one else to answer for it. Post-funding, that direct cause-and-effect relationship begins to blur. Your actions are now interpreted not just for their outcomes but for what they signal about your judgment, your alignment with the agreed strategy, and your ability to manage at scale.

This change in context demands a shift from reactive to intentional leadership. A scrappy founder's reflexes—moving fast, seizing every opportunity, cutting corners to accelerate delivery—are honed for scarcity. In a well-capitalised environment, those same instincts can become liabilities. A sudden influx of capital can tempt even disciplined leaders into overconfidence. The psychological relief of having "made it" financially can breed a dangerous complacency, leading to hires made for optics rather than capability, product expansions without market validation, or infrastructure investments driven by ambition rather than necessity. Such moves are rarely malicious; they are the product of a mindset that has not caught up with the new reality. *Capital changes the operating environment in ways that require a fundamentally different form of discipline—one rooted not in fear of failure, but in respect for complexity.*

One of the most significant psychological adjustments is learning to decouple personal worth from control over every decision. The scrappy founder often thrives on being indispensable, on having a hand in every critical choice. Investor capital complicates this because it brings with it both resources to delegate and the expectation that you will. Investors back founders to lead, not to hoard authority. A capital steward recognises that retaining control over too much not only slows the organisation but also sends a message of insecurity. The most effective leaders post-funding are those who can identify which levers they must personally hold, which can be delegated with trust, and which should be influenced indirectly through culture and strategic framing.

This is easier said than done. Delegation in the post-funding world is not merely a function of trust in your team—it is also a matter of governance. Investor capital often comes with formal oversight structures: boards, committees, mandated reporting, and performance milestones. Where the scrappy founder's power was largely informal and unchallenged, the capital steward operates in a context where certain decisions are no longer theirs to make unilaterally. Strategic pivots, major hires, and significant budget allocations may now require consultation, approval, or at the very least, advance notification. For founders accustomed to speed and autonomy, this can feel like a brake applied to the engine. Yet it is in this moment that the difference between resentment and adaptation determines the company's trajectory.

Adaptation does not mean surrendering vision; it means reframing leadership as the art of alignment. This involves not only shaping decisions to serve the business but also anticipating how those decisions will be perceived by stakeholders with different incentives. Investors, even when supportive, will inevitably filter your choices through their own priorities—whether it be timing for a future round, positioning for acquisition, or alignment with sector trends. The capital steward's role is to ensure these perspectives inform, but do not dictate, the company's strategic direction. That balance requires emotional maturity, a tolerance for scrutiny, and the ability to articulate a rationale that resonates across audiences.

There is also a subtler psychological shift that is often overlooked: moving from an existential focus on *survival* to a disciplined pursuit of *durability*. Scarcity forces focus; abundance demands selectivity. When cash was scarce, you were forced to make hard trade-offs because there was no alternative. With capital in hand, the pressure to choose carefully remains, but now the discipline must come from principle rather than necessity. This is where self-sabotage often occurs—when founders, unaccustomed to abundance, pursue every "good" opportunity without recognising that in the post-funding world, "good" is often the enemy of "essential." A capital steward understands that the cost of distraction is amplified by scale: a misaligned initiative can consume millions before its flaws become visible.

Consider the example of a fintech founder who, after raising a sizeable growth round, doubled the engineering team within three months to tackle three new product lines simultaneously. On paper, it was a bold expansion; in reality, it was an operational strain that diluted focus, delayed delivery, and ultimately alienated the very customer base that had fuelled their early success. Contrast this with a SaaS founder who, faced with similar investor enthusiasm for expansion, deliberately delayed a new product launch to strengthen core infrastructure, ensuring that when growth did come, it was supported by systems capable of sustaining it. The difference lay not in vision but in pacing—and pacing is a hallmark of stewardship.

The shift also has an internal dimension: the founder's relationship with self-perception. In the scrappy phase, identity is often intertwined with defying odds. You are the underdog, the one who refuses to quit. Post-funding, that narrative no longer fits. You are now, at least externally, a player with resources, credibility, and the backing of influential stakeholders. This can create a dissonance between how you see yourself and how the market now sees you. Some founders struggle to let go of the scrappy identity, clinging to start-up chaos as proof of authenticity. Others swing too far in the opposite direction, adopting a corporate polish that alienates the team and erodes the culture that drew talent in the first place. The effective capital steward integrates both identities: retaining the agility and hunger of the early stage while embracing the rigour and discipline the new phase demands.

Such integration requires conscious self-leadership. It is about cultivating habits that support clarity under pressure: structured decision-making processes, regular self-audit of priorities, and the ability to differentiate between investor influence that strengthens strategy and influence that dilutes it. It also means being alert to ego traps—taking on projects to impress rather than to advance the mission, or resisting governance processes purely as a matter of pride. *The most resilient founders recognise that their value is not in how much they do, but in how well they channel the organisation's energy toward the outcomes that matter most.*

Ultimately, the move from scrappy founder to capital steward is less about replacing one identity with another and more about evolving into a leader who can operate across contexts without losing coherence. It is about recognising that capital is not a windfall to be spent, but a resource to be multiplied; that investors are not merely backers but partners whose trust must be earned continually; and that leadership in this phase is measured not by survival, but by the ability to create enduring value in an environment where expectations are higher, stakes are larger, and the margin for error is smaller. The founders who master this shift not only protect their companies from avoidable crises—they position themselves to lead with authority, integrity, and strategic foresight long after the novelty of fresh funding has worn off.

The New Power Dynamics

The moment a funding deal closes, the nature of the founder–investor relationship changes in ways that are often invisible to those outside the table, but deeply felt by those within it. Before the deal, the relationship is largely courtship: the founder is selling a vision, the investor is evaluating risk and potential, and both sides retain the option to walk away. After the money lands, the dynamic shifts from evaluation to entanglement. Capital is no longer hypothetical—it is deployed, and with it comes a shared fate. That shared fate is not a perfect partnership of equals. It is a rebalancing of influence, authority, and expectations that requires a founder to quickly grasp the new rules of engagement.

The most immediate shift is psychological rather than contractual. In the pre-funding phase, an investor's perception of the founder is shaped by potential: the boldness of the idea, the charisma of the pitch, the ingenuity of the scrappy operation. Post-funding, perception becomes anchored to performance. Every board meeting, product update, and market movement is interpreted as evidence of whether their bet was wise. This change in lens transforms casual conversations into micro-assessments. A founder's ability to manage that perception—without becoming enslaved to it—becomes as important as their ability to manage operations.

The shift in expectations is equally profound. Investors who once applauded the founder's resourcefulness may now prioritise predictability. While early-stage improvisation is tolerated—even admired—it is replaced in the post-funding phase by an expectation of deliberate, data-backed decision-making. This does not mean investors lose their appetite for bold moves; rather, they expect boldness to be accompanied by defensible logic and a clear line of sight to impact. The founder who fails to recognise this recalibration can quickly find themselves labelled as undisciplined, even if they are making the same types of decisions that won investor confidence during the pitch process. *What changes is not the founder's instinct, but the lens through which that instinct is judged.*

Decision-making authority also undergoes a subtle but powerful transformation. The legal structure of most funding deals introduces governance mechanisms—board seats, veto rights, information covenants—that did not exist before. On paper, the founder may still have operational control. In practice, the presence of investor oversight alters the decision-making environment. Significant strategic moves—entering a new market, acquiring a competitor, overhauling the business model—are now often subject to pre-discussion, alignment, and sometimes explicit approval. For founders accustomed to unilateral action, this can feel like a constraint. Yet the more pragmatic view is that these structures, while limiting in speed, can enhance decision quality by introducing perspectives and expertise the founder may lack. The key is to treat governance as a forum for strategic sharpening, not as an obstacle to be navigated around.

Communication is the lever through which these new dynamics are managed. Pre-funding, updates tend to be occasional and curated—designed to build confidence and momentum. Post-funding, the cadence, depth, and tone of communication become part of the governance infrastructure. Investors expect regular, structured updates, not only on metrics but on risks, decision rationales, and forward-looking priorities. They want to be informed before surprises occur, not after. How these updates are crafted matters: a report that is purely factual can come across as cold or detached, while one that is overly promotional risks being read as spin. The most effective founders develop a communication style that is *transparent without being alarmist, strategic without being evasive*, and tailored to the individual temperaments of their investors.

These differences in temperament can be a source of friction if not understood. Not all investors view their role the same way. Some see themselves as sparring partners, probing weaknesses to strengthen the plan. Others prefer to act as connectors, opening doors to customers, hires, or future funding rounds. A few adopt a hands-off approach unless performance falters. Misalignment arises when founders assume a uniform approach or fail to clarify these working styles early on. Without that clarity, a perfectly normal strategic disagreement can be misinterpreted as hostility, or a lack of day-to-day engagement can be read as disinterest. The capital steward's task is to map these differences, adapt their interactions accordingly, and prevent small misreadings from calcifying into mistrust.

The new power dynamics are not static; they evolve with performance. A company that consistently meets or exceeds its milestones will often see investors adopt a more deferential stance, granting greater operational latitude. Conversely, missed targets—especially in consecutive periods—can tilt the balance towards increased scrutiny and influence. This is not purely punitive; it is a rational re-weighting of involvement when the original assumptions behind the investment appear at risk. For the founder, the challenge is to manage these cycles without letting them erode confidence internally. Overreaction to investor pressure can destabilise a team, just as ignoring legitimate concerns can fracture the board relationship.

Real-world cases underline the point. A consumer goods founder, after closing a major growth round, continued to run marketing experiments without prior board consultation, arguing that speed was the company's competitive edge. While the campaigns delivered short-term gains, they also triggered operational bottlenecks and strained inventory. The board's patience wore thin, not because the founder's instinct was wrong, but because the scale of risk had grown beyond what could be justified without formal oversight. Contrast this with a B2B software founder who used their first post-funding board meeting to lay out three strategic options for the next eighteen months, complete with risk assessments and capital implications. By involving investors in the decision framework early, they secured not just approval but active advocacy for the chosen path. The lesson: involvement is not surrender; it is strategic alignment.

Perhaps the most underappreciated aspect of the post-funding power shift is its asymmetry in reversibility. Investors can increase their influence relatively easily—by invoking governance rights, applying performance pressure, or signalling doubt in subtle ways that ripple through the company's ecosystem. Founders, on the other hand, find it much harder to reclaim influence once ceded. This makes the early months after funding critical for setting norms. How you handle the first disagreements, the first missed targets, the first strategic pivots, will shape the long-term tenor of the relationship.

None of this should be read as a warning against investor involvement; indeed, engaged investors often provide the relationships, credibility, and expertise that make the difference between moderate and breakout success. The point is that involvement is no longer optional. Once the cheque clears, the investor is not simply on your side—they are *inside* your business. The lines of influence are more fluid than the organisational chart suggests, and the founder who masters this reality gains an advantage that is as strategic as any market insight. They understand that the post-funding relationship is a constant act of calibration: between independence and interdependence, between vision and accountability, between the freedom to act and the wisdom to align.

The founders who navigate this with the greatest skill are those who recognise the shift early and adapt their stance accordingly. They neither retreat into defensive autonomy nor capitulate to every investor suggestion. Instead, they establish themselves as the central node in a network of influence—listening actively, engaging constructively, and making it clear that while capital has bought a seat at the table, it has not bought the table itself. In doing so, they preserve their ability to lead decisively while benefiting from the very forces that, if left unmanaged, could have eroded their authority.

From Autonomy to Accountability

For the founder, the shift from absolute decision-making authority to shared governance is not simply a procedural change; it is a recalibration of identity and power. Before external capital enters the picture, a founder operates with near-total autonomy. They decide what to build, when to launch, whom to hire, and how to allocate resources, guided by instinct and the immediate demands of survival. This freedom is intoxicating, and in many ways, it is essential to early-stage momentum—speed often trumps consensus when resources are scarce and opportunities fleeting. But the very act of accepting outside investment rewrites the decision-making architecture. The founder remains the chief executive, but now operates within a framework of oversight, accountability, and shared authority with a board whose composition they do not fully control.

This transition is jarring because it collides with the founder's formative leadership habits. In the pre-funding stage, agility and unilateral decision-making are not just traits—they are survival tools. Rapid pivots, bold bets, and rule-bending manoeuvres are rewarded when the only stakeholders are the team and the customers. Post-funding, those same traits can be reframed as recklessness, particularly when significant sums of capital are at stake. A strategic gamble that once required a brief internal discussion may now demand a board presentation, risk assessment, and investor sign-off. The founder must come to terms with the fact that *having the right answer is no longer enough; securing alignment around that answer is now part of the job.*

The presence of a board, especially one with investor representation, introduces a new layer of political and strategic complexity. The board's role is not to run the company day-to-day, but it does have legal and fiduciary obligations that give it influence over major decisions. Even when the founder retains a majority of voting rights, the psychological effect of regular scrutiny changes the dynamics of leadership. Every decision is now made with an awareness of how it will be perceived by those who have both capital and governance leverage. This is not inherently negative—effective boards can sharpen strategy and act as a bulwark against blind spots—but it requires the founder to master the art of *collaborative authority*, a skill that is rarely developed in the zero-sum environment of early start-up life.

One of the most challenging aspects of this shift is the erosion of unilateral control over strategic priorities. Where once the founder could dictate the balance between short-term revenue and long-term product development, they must now accommodate investor expectations about growth velocity, market positioning, and exit potential. The tension arises when these perspectives diverge: a founder may believe that slowing down to rebuild infrastructure is the prudent move, while the board might view it as a missed window of opportunity. In such moments, governance becomes not just a process of decision-making, but a negotiation over the company's very definition of success.

The emotional weight of this change should not be underestimated. Founders often experience a subtle but persistent sense of displacement. Their creation is no longer entirely theirs to steer, and the knowledge that major decisions require persuasion rather than proclamation can trigger defensiveness. Some respond by withdrawing—minimising board interaction to preserve a sense of independence—while others overcompensate, flooding the board with detail in an attempt to demonstrate competence. Both extremes are counterproductive. Withholding engagement risks eroding trust; overexposure can create unnecessary scrutiny. The founders who navigate this phase most effectively understand that *accountability does not have to diminish autonomy if managed with intention.*

The skill lies in building a governance rhythm that reinforces trust rather than tension. This means being deliberate about which issues warrant early board involvement and which can be resolved internally before presentation. It means framing decisions not as faits accomplis but as reasoned proposals, showing how risks have been evaluated and mitigated. The goal is to cultivate a pattern where the board sees the founder as both decisive and collaborative—capable of leading independently but willing to engage when the stakes demand it. This balance not only preserves operational agility but also strengthens the founder's standing when disagreements inevitably arise.

Real-world examples reveal the divergence in outcomes when this balance is struck—or missed. A mobility start-up founder, newly flush with Series B funding, continued to approve rapid city launches without prior board discussion, citing the need for competitive speed. When logistical bottlenecks emerged, the board's frustration was less about the problems themselves than the fact that they were blindsided by them. The resulting loss of confidence narrowed the founder's decision-making latitude for months. By contrast, a health-tech founder facing a critical regulatory decision convened an unscheduled board session to present three possible courses of action, each with clear cost-benefit analysis. The board backed the founder's preferred option unanimously, and the proactive engagement became a reference point for trust in future decisions.

The challenge is magnified by the different time horizons at play. Founders tend to think in terms of building a product and a company over years, sometimes decades; investors, particularly those operating under fund cycles, often have liquidity timelines measured in five to ten years. These differences inevitably colour the discussion of priorities, risk tolerance, and acceptable trade-offs. Shared governance means finding common ground between these timelines without allowing one to dominate in ways that compromise the company's viability or mission. This is where the founder's role evolves from decision-maker to *translator of priorities*, ensuring that long-term strategy is articulated in terms that satisfy near-term accountability.

This evolution also demands a recalibration of ego. In the autonomy phase, a founder's authority comes from being the central node through which all decisions pass. In the accountability phase, authority is maintained not by centralising every choice, but by demonstrating the judgment to know when to lead unilaterally, when to seek counsel, and when to defer. This can be uncomfortable, especially for founders whose self-image is rooted in being indispensable. Yet in high-functioning governance environments, the founder's influence is measured less by how many decisions they control and more by how consistently their leadership inspires confidence in those around the table.

Shared governance is not a dilution of leadership—it is an expansion of its scope. The founder now leads not just a company, but a coalition of stakeholders with intersecting interests and varying degrees of power. This requires political acuity, emotional intelligence, and a tolerance for ambiguity. It means recognising that a boardroom disagreement is not a personal attack but part of a system designed to manage risk and guide the company toward collective goals. It also means accepting that transparency, even when uncomfortable, is often the surest path to preserving both trust and influence.

The shift from autonomy to accountability is one of the most defining transitions in a founder's career. It tests not only their strategic acumen but their adaptability, self-awareness, and capacity for collaborative leadership under scrutiny. Those who master it emerge with more than just a funded company; they gain the resilience and political fluency to lead in environments where authority is always negotiated, never assumed. In a landscape where capital comes with expectations as tangible as the cash itself, learning to thrive in shared governance is not a concession—it is a prerequisite for enduring leadership.

Case in Point: The Scale-Up Shock

The first months after a major funding round are often framed as a victory lap, yet for many founders, they are the beginning of the most disorienting phase of leadership. The influx of capital changes the pace, scale, and scrutiny of operations overnight. Decisions that were once reversible experiments become costly commitments. Teams expand faster than culture can adapt. Market moves attract competitors' attention earlier than anticipated. This phenomenon—the scale-up shock—is not the result of inadequate intelligence or flawed ambition, but of underestimating how quickly the operating context transforms when abundance replaces scarcity. Real-world accounts illustrate that thriving in this phase requires not only strategy but a deep recalibration of leadership behaviour.

Consider the story of Lena M., founder of a B2B analytics platform that had bootstrapped to a respectable £2 million annual recurring revenue. Her team was lean, her product tightly focused, and her decision-making almost entirely instinctive. After closing a £15 million Series A led by a top-tier European VC, Lena moved quickly to capitalise on the momentum. Within four months, she had doubled headcount, opened two international offices, and expanded the product roadmap to include features her new investors believed could capture a broader market. On paper, it was an aggressive but plausible play. In practice, it destabilised the company's core. Engineering velocity slowed under the weight of additional priorities, customer support became fragmented across time zones, and the new hires—many of whom had been brought in under pressure to scale quickly—struggled to integrate into a culture that had been defined by tight-knit resourcefulness. The tipping point came when Lena was forced to delay a major launch, triggering investor concerns and a cascade of internal morale issues. What had been framed as the start of a growth chapter became an extended period of operational triage.

Lena's experience is not unusual. The speed at which capital demands to be put to work can outstrip a founder's ability to deliberately pace expansion. The board wanted to see the company "pull forward" its growth curve, and the incentives of the funding model encouraged rapid scaling as a hedge against competition. The oversight was in assuming that organisational infrastructure—management capacity, process maturity, and cultural coherence—would evolve at the same rate as headcount and market ambition. It rarely does. *The lesson is not that rapid scaling is inherently flawed, but that expansion without parallel strengthening of the operating core turns growth into a destabilising force rather than a compounding one.*

Contrast Lena's experience with that of Samir K., founder of a health-tech venture specialising in remote patient monitoring. After raising £20 million in a Series B, Samir resisted immediate pressure to launch into new international markets. Instead, he used the capital to professionalise the company's operational backbone—hiring an experienced COO, implementing scalable data infrastructure, and deepening clinical partnerships in existing geographies. To outside observers, this looked conservative, even timid. But when a regulatory change in the UK created an opportunity for rapid adoption, Samir's company was able to execute flawlessly, capturing a dominant market position before competitors could respond. His board, initially impatient with his deliberate approach, later cited it as the reason the company avoided the fate of other health-tech firms that overextended and collapsed under compliance burdens. Here, the scale-up shock was absorbed because the leadership understood that investor timelines could be negotiated if accompanied by a clear, defensible rationale for pacing.

Not all cases resolve positively. The cautionary example of fintech start-up VeridianPay demonstrates how mismanaging post-funding expectations can spiral. After securing a $30 million Series A from a consortium of US and Asian investors, the founder, Darren L., committed to a multi-product strategy intended to position the company as a "full-stack" solution. This pivot deviated sharply from the company's proven core competency in cross-border payments but was driven by investor enthusiasm for capturing adjacent markets. The board approved significant spend on marketing and engineering to support this vision. Within a year, the burn rate had exceeded projections by 40%, customer acquisition costs had doubled, and the flagship new product was six months behind schedule. When Darren returned to the board requesting bridge financing to extend runway, the investor mood had shifted; the additional capital was contingent on bringing in an external CEO.

Darren stayed on as Chief Product Officer but later admitted that his inability to push back on investor-driven scope expansion had cost him both strategic control and his role.

Darren's story underscores the delicate balance of agency in the post-funding environment. A founder may retain the title of CEO, but without a clear framework for managing investor influence, they risk being steered into strategies that align more with portfolio theory than with the operational realities of their company. Scale-up shock amplifies this risk because the urgency to show traction can make long-term trade-offs harder to defend. *When growth targets are set against investor expectations rather than organisational readiness, the probability of structural overreach rises sharply.*

It would be a mistake, however, to frame scale-up shock solely as a cautionary tale. In some instances, the jolt of post-funding intensity acts as a catalyst for leadership evolution. Take the case of Rina S., co-founder of an AI-powered logistics optimisation company. After raising £10 million, Rina recognised her own limitations in managing large-scale enterprise sales. Rather than attempting to learn on the job under investor scrutiny, she recruited a seasoned CRO from a multinational competitor. This decision, while emotionally challenging—effectively ceding a major function she had personally developed—enabled the company to land contracts that doubled its revenue in under a year. The combination of fresh capital and targeted leadership augmentation meant the scale-up phase was not only survivable but transformative.

What differentiates founders who thrive under scale-up shock from those who falter is not simply operational skill but the ability to *reframe the shock as a governance challenge rather than a purely operational one.* Thriving requires anticipating that the speed, scope, and visibility of decisions will increase exponentially—and building decision-making structures that can handle this without eroding cultural or strategic cohesion. It means being clear with investors about the sequencing of growth initiatives and having the data and narrative to defend that sequencing when pressure mounts. It also requires humility to recognise when the skills that served you well in the zero-to-one phase are no longer the ones that will protect and multiply post-funding gains.

The common thread across these cases is that scale-up shock is less about the presence of capital than the shift in tempo it imposes. The founder's challenge is to ensure that acceleration does not outpace absorption—that the organisation's systems, people, and market positioning can sustain the increased load. Misalignment between these elements leads to fragility; alignment creates the conditions for compounding advantage. The reality is that no founder is immune to the disorientation of scale-up shock. What matters is whether they enter this phase with the foresight to shape its impact rather than simply react to it. Those who do can turn what is often a destabilising jolt into a defining inflection point in the life of their company.

Chapter 2
Capital Is Not Cash Flow

The sight of a freshly funded bank account can be intoxicating in ways that are almost misleading. For a founder who has spent months—or even years—navigating survival on a threadbare budget, the sudden arrival of millions in fresh capital feels like liberation. Constraints that once dictated every decision loosen. Conversations that ended with "we can't afford it" now begin with "how quickly can we make this happen?" The relief is real, and yet, so too is the hidden risk. Capital, regardless of its magnitude, is not synonymous with cash flow. It is finite, time-bound, and exists to be converted into sustainable revenue. Confusing the two is one of the fastest ways to trade solvency for scarcity in the post-funding phase.

The allure of abundance is particularly seductive because it preys upon a founder's ingrained scarcity mindset. When every penny once carried weight, each expenditure was deliberate; priorities were ruthlessly ordered. Post-funding, that friction evaporates. Suddenly, the company finds itself saying "yes" with ease: yes to hiring multiple senior hires simultaneously, yes to parallel product lines, yes to bold marketing campaigns without rigorous ROI analysis. The logic seems sound—after all, isn't acceleration the whole point of raising capital? Yet acceleration without a disciplined deployment plan is velocity without direction. A business can move quickly in precisely the wrong direction when financial signals are distorted by a one-off cash injection. The mere presence of money shifts decision-making bias, inflating confidence in capacity while underestimating risk.

This tension is most acute when founders consider runway and burn rate. Often treated as static metrics—a simple calculation of months until funds run out—they are, in truth, highly dynamic. Hiring decisions, market shifts, acquisition costs, and operational surprises all compress or extend runway in real time. Investor forecasts present a tidy, linear picture: eighteen months of runway, eighteen months of breathing room. Reality is messier. Competitors cut prices aggressively, regulatory obligations crop up unexpectedly, key customers churn. The founder's role is not merely to know the number but to actively manage it—modulating spend according to performance, opportunity, and risk.

Paradoxically, large sums of capital can act more like constraints than freedoms. Accepting a major funding round comes with implicit expectations: growth targets, revenue milestones, and pacing set by investors. These expectations narrow strategic flexibility. A founder might prefer to consolidate market position or refine product-market fit but finds themselves compelled to pursue aggressive expansion to stay in alignment with the funding narrative. The pressure intensifies when valuations are ambitious: higher multiples demand steeper growth curves, leaving little room to adjust course without signalling weakness.

The remedy is a deliberate capital deployment plan. This is not a mere budget; it is a strategic blueprint linking every pound spent to measurable outcomes and forward momentum. It spells out the sequence of investments: which hires accelerate revenue milestones, which product initiatives secure market defensibility, which operational improvements reduce future burn. Discipline here is less about austerity than intention—deploying capital in ways that compound impact rather than dissipate it.

The psychological high of funding often masks the need for such discipline. Consider a founder who launches an expansive marketing blitz immediately post-funding. Brand awareness spikes, inbound leads surge, yet customer acquisition costs balloon beyond payback assumptions. Without concurrent investment in conversion optimisation, onboarding capacity, and retention, gains remain shallow. By the time this becomes evident, burn has permanently ratcheted upward, compressing runway and forcing reactive cuts that erode morale. Contrast this with a founder who sequences deployment: piloting campaigns locally, iterating based on early performance, then scaling with a proven model. Early progress may seem slower, but its compounding effect on sustainable growth far surpasses the one-off blitz.

Capital also brings internal pressures. As headcount rises, so too does the temptation to allocate resources evenly across departments, sometimes driven more by politics than strategic value. A rigorous deployment plan anchors decisions in company-wide priorities rather than internal optics. Leadership must combine financial literacy with the courage to communicate spending rationales clearly—even when that requires saying no to popular initiatives.

At a philosophical level, capital should be treated not as fuel but as a catalyst. Fuel is consumed; catalysts amplify transformation without unnecessary depletion. A fuel mentality spends until the tank runs dry, relying on the next round to refill it. A catalyst mentality deploys funds to generate self-sustaining cash flow, transforming a temporary advantage into a lasting one.

In the pages ahead, we will unravel the myth that capital itself equals financial strength. We will examine the psychological biases that distort spending post-funding, explore strategies to extend runway without halting momentum, and outline frameworks that tie allocation to measurable, strategic outcomes. The goal is to equip founders with both mindset and methods, ensuring every pound of investor capital strengthens—not weakens—the company's capacity to generate enduring value. True stewardship is measured not by speed of spend but by the deliberate conversion of investor funds into compounding, self-sustaining growth.

The Illusion of Abundance

The most dangerous financial position a founder can be in is not when the bank account is nearly empty, but when it has just been filled. Scarcity has a way of enforcing discipline—every hire is weighed against opportunity cost, every vendor contract is negotiated with rigour, every expansion plan is scrutinised for its immediate payback. Abundance, by contrast, relaxes the constraints that sharpen judgement. The numbers on the account statement suggest security, but in a start-up context, that security is often a mirage. It is not income; it is finite capital, front-loaded and non-renewable unless converted into revenue. Yet psychologically, having a large sum available can alter decision-making in subtle and dangerous ways, creating a false sense of capacity and permanence.

This shift in mindset happens faster than most founders expect. Before funding, internal discussions about spending tend to begin with "Can we afford this?" After funding, they often start with "Should we try this?"—a seemingly minor change in language that signals a much larger shift in decision-making posture. When money feels plentiful, the burden of proof for spending decisions lightens. Initiatives are greenlit not because they are mission-critical but because they are possible. *The presence of capital reduces the perceived cost of experimentation, but not the actual cost.* A product line that absorbs £500,000 without producing revenue is no less damaging to runway simply because the capital was raised rather than earned.

There is a particular psychological distortion that occurs when new capital is framed as "runway" rather than as "capital to be invested for return." In the founder's mind, runway is time—time to experiment, time to build, time to prove. But every month of burn is a depletion of optionality. Unless that burn is accompanied by proportional growth in revenue or valuation, each passing month is, in effect, a narrowing of future choices. The illusion of abundance makes it easy to treat time as if it were replenishable simply by raising the next round, ignoring the fact that future funding will be contingent on how effectively this capital is deployed now.

Real-world cases illustrate how quickly this illusion can turn corrosive. A direct-to-consumer fashion start-up, flush with $25 million in Series B funding, decided to expand into three international markets simultaneously. Their pre-funding operations had been laser-focused, with a small, agile team and a single distribution centre. Post-funding, they leased multiple regional offices, hired local marketing teams, and contracted with new logistics partners—all within six months. The expansion consumed resources at a rate that outpaced sales growth, and when currency fluctuations hit one of the new markets, losses spiralled. Within eighteen months, the company was forced to pull back to its core geography, having burned more than half its capital on a failed scale-up. The founder later admitted that, without the large cash reserve, the decision to expand so broadly would never have passed an internal cost–benefit analysis.

The distortion does not only affect strategy; it reshapes culture. Before funding, teams are used to operating with a degree of frugality that fosters creativity. Constraints force prioritisation. Post-funding, departments begin to operate as though capital allocation is a given rather than a competitive process. Leaders start building ideal-state budgets instead of stripped-down, essentials-first plans. Over time, the organisational metabolism speeds up—not necessarily in output, but in the rate at which resources are consumed. This is one reason why founders often find their burn rate rising faster than planned without any corresponding leap in performance metrics. *Money does not just enable growth—it can enable waste at scale if not actively managed.*

The illusion is reinforced by the way success is signalled in the start-up ecosystem. Funding rounds are celebrated as if they were revenue milestones. Media coverage, internal morale, and industry recognition all spike when capital is raised, creating a subconscious association between raising money and winning. The danger is that this external validation can subtly shift internal priorities—from building enduring revenue streams to managing the optics of growth. When the goal becomes to justify the size of the raise rather than to deploy it for maximum strategic return, spending decisions can begin to serve narrative needs over business needs.

It is also worth recognising that the illusion of abundance is not purely self-generated; it is sometimes encouraged by investors themselves. The venture model is built on accelerating growth to maximise returns within fund lifecycles, and there is a natural bias towards spending to achieve speed. A founder who resists this may feel they are being overly cautious, even when prudence is warranted. Here lies the tension: the investor's portfolio is diversified, but the founder's exposure is concentrated. Reckless spending in pursuit of portfolio-level outcomes may still be rational for the investor but devastating for the founder if it undermines the company's survival. Navigating this requires the confidence to push back when spending proposals are misaligned with operational readiness, backed by data that reframes restraint as a growth strategy rather than a lack of ambition.

The solution is not austerity for its own sake, but intentionality. One of the most effective ways to counter the illusion of abundance is to mentally reclassify the capital in the bank. Instead of treating it as a lump sum available for discretionary spending, allocate it into defined strategic pools tied to specific milestones—product readiness, market entry, customer acquisition thresholds. This mental and operational framing restores the sense of scarcity where it matters most, forcing trade-offs and prioritisation even in the presence of cash. It also makes the true opportunity cost of every pound spent visible: if a £250,000 marketing experiment comes from a clearly defined pool, the trade-off against other initiatives becomes tangible.

The founders who manage to pierce the illusion early tend to share certain traits. They are sceptical of their own instincts when flush with capital, running spending decisions through the same rigour they applied before funding. They build dashboards that track not just cash burn but the efficiency of every significant spend category, allowing them to detect early signs of diminishing returns. They foster cultures where frugality is not equated with lack of ambition, but with respect for the value of optionality. Most importantly, they view capital as a tool to buy control over timing and strategy—not as a cushion to delay hard decisions.

In truth, abundance is never as abundant as it appears. Every pound in the bank after a funding round is already spoken for in some way—by payroll commitments, by infrastructure needs, by the capital intensity of the next growth phase. The danger lies in treating what is essentially earmarked capital as if it were free cash flow. Without discipline, the illusion becomes reality all too quickly: the company finds itself in the same position it started—cash constrained—only now with a higher cost base, a shorter runway, and less room to manoeuvre. The founders who survive and thrive are those who refuse to let the presence of money dull their sharpness, knowing that the discipline forged in scarcity is just as vital in abundance—if not more so.

Runway vs. Burn Rate

One of the most sobering realisations for a newly funded founder is that a healthy bank balance is not the same as a healthy financial position. Cash in the bank is a static number; the company's burn rate and runway together determine whether that number represents stability, fragility, or a rapidly approaching crisis. Yet too often, founders rely on investor forecasts as if they were weather reports—treated as authoritative but rarely examined for their assumptions. The result is a dangerous complacency that assumes the trajectory is fixed when, in fact, runway is one of the most fluid and founder-controlled metrics in the business. *Mastering the interplay between burn rate and runway is not a finance department exercise—it is a core discipline of post-funding leadership.*

Runway, in its simplest definition, is the amount of time a company has before it runs out of cash at its current burn rate. Burn rate, meanwhile, is the net amount of cash leaving the business each month after accounting for all inflows and outflows. The arithmetic is basic: divide available cash by monthly burn to calculate months remaining. But the simplicity of the formula hides a critical truth—both the numerator and denominator are constantly moving targets. Available cash changes with customer payments, investment tranches, and unforeseen expenses; burn rate fluctuates with hiring decisions, marketing campaigns, seasonality, and operational hiccups. Treating either figure as fixed is a strategic error.

Founders often underestimate how quickly burn rate can accelerate. A single round of senior hires, a shift to larger office space, or the decision to enter a new market can raise monthly burn by double digits. Once those costs are embedded, they are difficult to reverse without morale-sapping cuts. Conversely, small, deliberate changes in spending can extend runway significantly, even without new revenue. The founder who understands these levers can treat burn rate as a controllable variable rather than a fixed consequence of growth. This is why the most effective leaders build not one runway projection, but several—best case, worst case, and likely case—each tied to specific assumptions about revenue, spend, and external conditions.

Investor forecasts tend to err on the optimistic side, often assuming linear revenue growth and a relatively stable burn profile. This is not inherently deceitful; it is a natural byproduct of fundraising, where models are designed to inspire confidence. But the founder's job is to stress-test those models under less forgiving assumptions. What happens if sales cycles lengthen by 30 days? If churn increases by a few percentage points? If hiring costs come in above projections? Running these scenarios is not an academic exercise; it is a way to pre-empt the erosion of runway before it becomes irreversible. *The ability to spot an approaching runway compression three quarters in advance rather than three months is often the difference between raising the next round from a position of strength and raising it under duress.*

Real-world examples bring this into sharper focus. A SaaS company that had raised $12 million was projecting an 18-month runway based on investor-approved forecasts. However, they had not accounted for the fact that their sales team's ramp-up time was longer than expected, meaning revenue growth would lag by two quarters. When the CFO recalculated runway using actuals instead of projections, they discovered they had just 12 months—not 18—before hitting zero. That six-month gap was the difference between entering the market for a Series B with strong metrics and scrambling for bridge financing. In contrast, another venture in the same sector regularly ran variance analyses between forecast and actuals, adjusting spending within the same quarter to preserve target runway. When their CAC (customer acquisition cost) temporarily spiked due to market saturation, they slowed planned hires in non-revenue-generating departments, keeping the burn rate aligned with their revised revenue trajectory.

Effective runway management requires seeing beyond the headline number of "months left" and understanding the underlying composition of burn. Not all expenses are equal in their relationship to growth. Some outflows directly drive revenue—sales commissions, targeted marketing campaigns, certain R&D investments—while others are structural or discretionary. A disciplined founder differentiates between *growth burn* and *maintenance burn.* Growth burn is intentional and tied to measurable returns; maintenance burn is the baseline cost of keeping the lights on. The danger arises when growth burn fails to deliver returns, yet spending continues as if it were still an investment rather than a sunk cost.

Another overlooked element is the *shape* of the runway. Two companies may each have 12 months of runway, but the risk profile is not the same if one expects a steep revenue ramp in the final quarter while the other maintains a steady upward trajectory from the next month onward. A back-loaded growth plan is inherently riskier because it compresses the margin for error—if market conditions delay that revenue ramp, the entire plan collapses into a liquidity crisis. Understanding the shape of the runway forces the founder to think about cash needs not just in aggregate, but in sequence.

Monitoring runway is not just a financial exercise—it is a communication tool. Boards and investors are more confident when a founder can discuss runway with precision, articulate the drivers of burn rate, and explain the specific levers available to extend it. Vague reassurances that "we have about a year" erode credibility; detailed discussions about how a hiring freeze in Q3 could add four months to runway, or how shifting marketing spend to higher-conversion channels could improve efficiency, signal control and foresight. The best founders frame runway conversations in terms of strategic options—demonstrating that they are not merely passengers in the financial trajectory of the business, but active pilots.

Philosophically, the discipline of managing runway forces a founder to confront the tension between ambition and prudence. Growth requires spending ahead of revenue, but overspending relative to validated traction shortens the strategic time horizon. In early-stage companies, time is not just a metric—it is the ultimate asset. The longer the runway, the more shots at refining product-market fit, the more flexibility to respond to competition, and the more control over fundraising timing. Shortening runway unnecessarily, even in pursuit of aggressive growth, is effectively trading control for speed—and control is much harder to regain once lost.

The interplay between burn rate and runway should be seen as a living dashboard, not a static report. It demands active monitoring, real-time adjustments, and scenario planning that challenges optimistic assumptions. Founders who master this do not think of runway as the time until money runs out; they think of it as the strategic breathing room that enables them to choose when and how to act. That reframing changes everything—from how budgets are built to how growth bets are placed. In the end, the companies that survive are not always those that raise the most, but those that spend with the clearest understanding of how each pound burned today shapes the strategic options available tomorrow.

Funding as a Growth Constraint

The counterintuitive truth of venture finance is that large sums of capital, while marketed as the fuel for freedom and expansion, can become a form of strategic handcuffs. The very act of accepting a substantial investment commits a founder to a growth trajectory that may not align with market realities, product maturity, or operational readiness. This paradox sits at the heart of many post-funding struggles: *capital amplifies opportunity, but it also hardens expectations*. Once the wire transfer clears, the financial narrative shifts. Growth is no longer optional—it becomes the central measure by which progress, competence, and leadership are judged.

For the investor, the logic is clear. Their model is built on achieving returns that outpace risk, which means capital must be deployed with urgency toward high-growth outcomes. A £20 million Series B is not provided to build resilience, experiment patiently, or optimise existing revenue streams—it is intended to accelerate expansion, often at a pace dictated by the investment thesis rather than the company's natural evolution. This is why, paradoxically, the moment the capital arrives is also the moment strategic flexibility begins to narrow. The founder, who once could pivot decisively in response to emerging data, now finds themselves operating within a framework of agreed milestones and growth targets that have been embedded into board expectations, investor updates, and future funding assumptions.

Consider the case of a retail technology startup that had built a strong regional presence, generating steady monthly growth through direct sales and partnerships. When they secured a large investment from a growth equity firm, the expectation was clear: national expansion within 18 months, followed by entry into two European markets. On paper, the funding provided the resources to hire aggressively, scale marketing, and open new locations. In practice, the pace of rollout outstripped the company's operational depth. Training pipelines couldn't keep up with hiring, quality control slipped, and the brand's reputation suffered in new markets. The capital, which could have been used to consolidate strengths and build a foundation for sustainable expansion, became a constraint by forcing an accelerated timetable that introduced strategic risk.

This phenomenon is not limited to operational strain. It extends to product strategy. A company with £10 million in the bank and a modest, steadily growing user base might, under founder-led decision-making, choose to refine core features, improve retention, and expand cautiously into adjacent markets. Once large-scale funding is in play, however, those priorities are often redefined. The product roadmap must justify the valuation that underpinned the raise, meaning launches are pushed forward, feature sets expand beyond validated demand, and marketing spend increases to meet ambitious adoption curves. What was once a deliberate product evolution becomes a race to hit numbers that may not reflect the company's organic path. *The pursuit of investor-aligned growth can, unintentionally, pull a business away from customer-aligned growth.*

There is also a psychological element to this shift. Founders often speak about "spending other people's money" with a mix of liberation and latent anxiety. The liberation comes from being able to take bolder bets without the existential fear of bankruptcy around the corner. The anxiety emerges when those bets are no longer chosen purely by the founder but are shaped by an implicit social contract with the investors. Even in the absence of formal restrictions, there is a powerful gravitational pull towards strategies that "look" like high-growth plays—large team expansions, high-profile partnerships, aggressive market entries—because these are the visible markers of momentum. The subtler, less photogenic work of building infrastructure, deepening customer relationships, and strengthening organisational culture can be harder to defend when the boardroom is calibrated to quarterly growth charts.

One of the more insidious constraints comes from the way large capital infusions redefine risk. In a bootstrapped or lightly funded environment, the cost of failure is immediate but contained; a failed experiment may slow growth, but the business can often recover through adjustment. With tens of millions committed, however, the cost of failure is magnified—not just financially, but reputationally. A high-profile setback can unsettle investors, derail future fundraising, and damage market confidence. This can lead founders to become more conservative in their decision-making at exactly the moment when they are expected to act boldly, creating a tension that hampers both agility and innovation.

The paradox is deepened by the signalling effect of large raises. Competitors interpret the funding as a declaration of intent and respond aggressively, accelerating their own timelines or launching counter-initiatives. The market environment becomes artificially heated, with rivals, talent, and even customers adjusting their expectations of the company's performance. The founder's strategic space narrows further—not because of explicit investor pressure, but because the broader ecosystem begins to interact with the business as though it were already a fully scaled player, erasing the margin for iterative learning that smaller firms enjoy.

This is not an argument against raising substantial capital—it is an argument for understanding the trade-offs it imposes. Founders who navigate this well tend to approach large raises with the same sceptical rigour they would apply to a major acquisition or partnership. They map not only the growth opportunities the capital will unlock, but also the commitments and constraints it will impose. They negotiate milestones that allow for adaptive execution rather than linear escalation. They maintain a portfolio of initiatives that balance high-return bets with foundational investments, ensuring that short-term acceleration does not undermine long-term resilience.

Philosophically, the core challenge is aligning the pace of growth with the company's capacity for sustainable execution. Market share gained through brute-force spending can evaporate if the underlying product, culture, or operational discipline lags behind. A founder's role, post-raise, is not simply to spend the capital efficiently, but to protect the strategic optionality that made the business valuable in the first place. *Large sums can buy speed, but they also compress the timeline in which strategic missteps can be corrected.* The irony is that the more capital a founder takes, the less room they may have to manoeuvre—unless they enter the deal with eyes wide open and a plan designed to defend flexibility as fiercely as they pursue growth.

Designing a Capital Deployment Plan

The availability of capital changes the psychology of decision-making as much as it changes the mathematics of a balance sheet. Without a deliberate plan, money can seep into every appealing opportunity and every well-intentioned initiative until the company's resources are spread too thin to create real impact. The founders who deploy capital most effectively treat it not as a windfall to be spent but as an instrument to be orchestrated, where every allocation serves a defined strategic objective and is tethered to measurable milestones. The discipline lies not in limiting spend for its own sake, but in ensuring that *each pound deployed brings the company closer to a state of demonstrably greater value.*

Effective capital deployment begins with clarity. Before any expenditure is committed, the leadership team must articulate the strategic outcomes that matter most over the funding cycle—whether that is capturing a defined share of a priority market, hitting specific product adoption thresholds, or reaching operational breakeven. These outcomes should be explicit enough to resist dilution under the pressure of new ideas, investor suggestions, or competitive moves. The absence of such clarity invites the kind of opportunistic spending that feels productive but delivers little compounding benefit. *Capital without purpose has a gravitational pull towards the urgent at the expense of the important.*

One proven approach is to reverse-engineer the deployment plan from clearly defined milestone events that will materially change the company's position—milestones that could trigger a higher valuation, unlock a new market, or create defensible competitive advantage. By working backwards from these points, leadership can determine the minimum viable resource allocation needed to achieve them, avoiding the trap of inflating budgets simply because more money is available. This method also acts as a safeguard against "nice-to-have" spending, ensuring that every cost line is directly associated with a strategic milestone and not just a functional wish list.

However, a well-constructed plan is not merely a set of budget categories with assigned amounts—it is a governance mechanism.

Capital deployment should be structured around periodic reviews, where performance against milestone-linked KPIs is evaluated before further funding is released to each initiative. This introduces an element of internal accountability that mirrors the investor's oversight function but keeps it within the founder's control. It also ensures that spending decisions remain dynamic and responsive, rather than locked in based on assumptions that may have aged poorly in the fast-moving environment of a scale-up.

Consider the example of a B2B SaaS company that raised £15 million to accelerate customer acquisition. Without a rigorous deployment plan, it might have channelled the bulk of the funds into a broad marketing push and rapid sales team expansion. Instead, the leadership identified two gating milestones: reducing onboarding friction to cut churn by 40%, and securing three anchor enterprise clients whose case studies could drive credibility. The capital deployment was sequenced to hit these milestones before scaling marketing spend. By resisting the impulse to spend heavily upfront, they maximised the impact of later investments, ensuring that increased acquisition was supported by retention capability and market validation.

A common tension in capital deployment planning is balancing offensive and defensive spending. Offensive spending—market expansion, product launches, brand campaigns—generates excitement and is often easier to justify in boardrooms seeking rapid returns. Defensive spending—improving infrastructure, upgrading security, strengthening compliance—may not generate immediate visible growth, but it preserves the company's capacity to scale without collapse. A sophisticated deployment plan acknowledges that both are essential and allocates proportionately to maintain long-term resilience alongside short-term momentum.

The temptation to overcommit to fixed costs is another hazard. New capital often prompts a hiring surge, the signing of long-term leases, or the commitment to expensive technology contracts. While these may be necessary in some cases, they lock the company into obligations that cannot easily be unwound if market conditions shift. A disciplined capital deployment plan builds flexibility into cost structures, favouring variable over fixed commitments wherever possible, so that adjustments can be made without destabilising the business. The most effective founders treat capital as a lever for optionality, not a ticket to irreversible expansion.

Philosophically, designing a capital deployment plan requires an acceptance that not every initiative will deliver the anticipated return, and that part of the founder's role is to cut losses decisively. Capital planning is not about spending every allocated pound to completion; it is about *continually reallocating towards the highest-yield opportunities based on real data.* This demands humility, discipline, and a willingness to deprioritise pet projects when they no longer serve the strategic path.

Ultimately, the strength of a capital deployment plan lies not in its initial perfection but in its adaptability. The best plans establish a clear strategic north star, allocate resources with precision to measurable milestones, and incorporate mechanisms for rapid reassessment. They protect against the two most dangerous forces after a funding round: the euphoria that encourages indiscriminate spending, and the inertia that prevents timely course correction. Capital, when deployed with intention and governed with discipline, becomes more than fuel—it becomes a force multiplier for strategy, amplifying not just the company's speed, but the quality and durability of its progress.

Chapter 3
The Investor Relationship Portfolio

Securing investment is often depicted as a neat pivot: the end of financial scarcity and the dawn of growth. In practice, however, it is far messier. A funding round is not simply a transactional exchange of money for equity—it inaugurates a complex, ongoing relationship. Investors arrive with their own histories, ambitions, and constraints. Some are driven chiefly by financial returns, scrutinising every decision through the lens of projected multiples. Others are motivated by strategic influence, seeking to shape your direction in ways that serve their broader portfolio or corporate objectives. Still others chase less tangible rewards: the prestige of backing innovation, the thrill of proximity to a pioneering sector, or the opportunity to be associated with a future market leader. For a founder, this diversity is not abstract theory—it defines the terrain upon which the company must navigate alignment, pre-empt missteps, and extract mutual value.

Too often, inexperienced founders treat investors as a monolith, assuming a single style of engagement will suffice. That assumption rarely holds. A venture capital partner managing a fund with a ten-year horizon faces very different pressures from a family office focused on generational wealth, or a strategic corporate investor whose product might complement—or compete with—your own. These differences shape tolerance for risk, appetite for reinvestment, and even definitions of success. Early recognition of these drivers—and managing them without compromising strategic autonomy—is essential. A founder must become fluent in the subtle, often unspoken language of investor motivations.

At the heart of every strong investor relationship lies information flow. It is tempting, especially during periods of growth, to limit updates to highlights and headline metrics. Yet investor confidence relies as much on the completeness and transparency of data as on the results themselves. Discipline in reporting—structured, context-rich, and data-supported—allows investors to follow the rationale behind decisions and anticipate potential issues before they escalate. The most effective founders construct an "information architecture," standardising cadence, content, and format. This is not mere administrative formality; it signals reliability, reinforces credibility, and positions the founder as a careful steward of both capital and strategy.

Advocacy is a frequently overlooked benefit of robust investor relationships. Many founders see investors primarily as financiers, occasionally as advisors, and only rarely as active amplifiers of the business. Yet the right investor can open doors: introductions to key customers, guidance navigating complex regulation, or informal endorsements that accelerate trust in competitive markets. The challenge lies in leveraging these advantages without creating dependency or surrendering strategic control. Successful founders ask targeted, high-impact questions that align with both company priorities and the investor's willingness to engage. When managed carefully, investors evolve from passive shareholders into multipliers of reach and credibility.

Conflict is unavoidable when money, ambition, and uncertainty intersect. The test of leadership is not the absence of disagreements, but how they are handled. Tensions may arise from divergent strategic visions, market fluctuations, operational setbacks, or interpersonal friction. The instinct to defend every decision can harden positions and erode trust. Composure—rooted in preparation, active listening, and separating ego from outcome—yields far better results. Founders who frame disputes around shared objectives and pursue resolutions that preserve alignment often emerge with relationships strengthened. Sometimes, one well-managed disagreement earns more respect than a year of unbroken good news.

This chapter treats the founder–investor relationship not as a static duty but as a living, evolving portfolio—requiring active management, diversified engagement, and periodic recalibration as the company's stage, strategy, and market conditions change. It demands strategic empathy: the ability to see through each investor's lens while retaining the conviction to lead in the company's best interest. By understanding motivations, creating reliable communication systems, harnessing advocacy judiciously, and navigating conflict with skill, founders can transform a fragile network of capital providers into a resilient source of strategic strength. The following pages offer practical frameworks, actionable tactics, and illustrative case studies to help you cultivate these enduring partnerships.

Different Investors, Different Agendas: Understanding the diversity of investor motivations—financial return, strategic influence, prestige—and why it matters for managing expectations

Capital rarely arrives without conditions, whether written in a shareholder agreement or woven silently into the psychology of the people behind the cheque. The assumption that all investors are motivated by the same end—maximising financial returns—is convenient but dangerously incomplete. In truth, the venture landscape is populated by actors whose goals can be as diverse as the companies they fund, and a founder who fails to read these motivations accurately risks not only strategic friction but, in some cases, the erosion of the company's independence. *Money may look identical once in the bank account, but the intent that follows it is anything but uniform.*

At one end of the spectrum lie investors driven by pure financial performance. These may be venture capital firms operating within the rigid timelines of a fund structure, private equity houses hunting for efficiency gains, or individual angels with a clear expectation of a multiple on their investment within a defined horizon. Their priority is capital growth, and their patience is tied directly to performance metrics. This group's focus on exit pathways, market share capture, and EBITDA improvement can be valuable in instilling operational discipline. Yet, it also creates a specific type of pressure: decisions will often be evaluated less by their strategic elegance than by their projected effect on valuation in the near term. This does not make them wrong—it makes them predictable. The founder's challenge is to align the company's growth path with these return expectations without distorting its underlying purpose.

A very different proposition is the strategic investor. This might be a corporate venture arm, a large supplier, or a distribution partner who sees the startup not as a standalone financial asset but as a tool to strengthen their core business. Their metrics for success may have little to do with the company's balance sheet. Instead, they might care about exclusivity arrangements, integration potential, or securing first access to innovation. This alignment can unlock opportunities—favourable contracts, industry credibility, faster market entry—that are hard to replicate through purely financial backers. But the bargain is double-edged: strategic investors may push for product roadmaps or market moves that serve their interests first, even if they diverge from the founder's long-term vision. The capacity to accept their capital while ring-fencing the company's autonomy is a delicate but vital skill.

Then there are investors whose motivations are largely intangible—those drawn by the prestige of association with innovation, the social capital of being seen as a patron of emerging talent, or the personal satisfaction of contributing to a transformative idea. This can include high-net-worth individuals, family offices, or philanthropically inclined funds. Their expectations may be less financially aggressive and more focused on narrative: they want to back something that makes them look astute, prescient, or principled. These relationships can be rich in patience and goodwill, but they carry their own subtleties. Reputation-driven investors may still demand influence over brand positioning, public communications, or governance in ways that reflect their desired public image. Disappoint them on these fronts, and their enthusiasm can wane as quickly as it appeared.

Most companies will, over time, accumulate a portfolio of investors spanning these motivations. The complexity lies in the interactions between them. A board meeting that includes a venture capitalist seeking a three-year exit, a corporate partner advocating for market exclusivity, and a prestige-driven patron eager for social impact metrics is a stage on which competing definitions of success play out in real time. The founder's role is to interpret and reconcile these agendas without alienating any stakeholder to the point of disengagement—or worse, obstruction. This is less about appeasement than about expectation design: setting clear terms for what the company can and cannot deliver to each type of investor and ensuring that commitments are matched to capabilities.

Expectation management begins long before capital is accepted. Too many founders treat due diligence as a one-way process, forgetting that they, too, must interrogate the investor's track record, decision-making style, and post-investment behaviour. What companies have they backed? How do they act when performance lags? Do they have a reputation for constructive involvement or for micromanagement? These questions are not academic—they are predictive. An investor's past conduct is often the best guide to their future demands, and entering a relationship without this intelligence is to trade the certainty of equity dilution for the uncertainty of strategic interference.

Once the relationship is underway, the key to balancing diverse agendas is disciplined communication. This does not mean treating all investors identically—it means tailoring information to their priorities without fragmenting the strategic narrative. A financial return–driven investor might be given sharper focus on unit economics, customer acquisition cost trends, and exit scenario modelling. A strategic investor might receive deeper insight into integration timelines, technology roadmaps, or market share metrics relevant to their sector. A prestige-driven investor might value stories that highlight brand leadership, media recognition, or societal impact. The sophistication lies in ensuring these tailored perspectives never contradict each other and all remain anchored to the company's central strategy.

There is also a deeper philosophical question that founders must confront: *to what extent should investor motivations shape the company's priorities at all?* In the early stages, when survival hinges on securing capital, the temptation to bend to the loudest or most powerful investor is acute. Yet, over the long term, a company whose strategy is the product of investor compromise rather than founder conviction often finds itself pursuing incoherent objectives. The founder's responsibility is to maintain a hierarchy of decision-making in which investor input is weighted and integrated, but not allowed to override the core mission or operational logic of the business.

The paradox of diverse investor agendas is that, managed well, they can strengthen the company by providing a multi-dimensional view of opportunities and risks. Each type of investor sees the world through a different lens, and this diversity, when channelled constructively, can prevent strategic blind spots. Managed poorly, it fractures governance, slows decision-making, and can even precipitate founder replacement. The difference between these outcomes rests on the founder's ability to *anticipate, interpret, and integrate*—to anticipate the motivations that will drive investor behaviour, to interpret their requests in light of those motivations, and to integrate their input into a coherent strategy that serves the company first.

In the end, capital is never neutral. Every pound or dollar accepted carries the weight of the ambitions, constraints, and values of the person or institution providing it. The founder who recognises this truth early is far better equipped to design relationships that endure pressure, harness influence productively, and align divergent agendas towards a shared outcome. Those who ignore it may find that the cost of capital is not measured in percentage points of equity, but in the erosion of control over the very enterprise they set out to build.

Information Architecture: How to structure reporting and updates that build confidence and pre-empt difficult conversations

The moment a founder secures capital, they also inherit an unspoken obligation: to keep their investors informed in a way that inspires confidence, not anxiety. Reporting is often misunderstood as a compliance exercise—a set of numbers and updates dispatched at agreed intervals. In reality, it is a strategic discipline, one that shapes investor perception, frames the company's trajectory, and determines the tone of every future conversation. *The way information is structured and delivered is not neutral; it can either invite constructive partnership or ignite unnecessary scrutiny.*

The challenge lies in striking the right balance between transparency and control. Too little information leaves investors uneasy, prone to filling gaps with assumptions. Too much information, especially when poorly structured, overwhelms them and risks drawing attention to noise rather than signal. The architecture of reporting is the founder's tool for controlling the narrative—not by obscuring the truth, but by framing it in a way that contextualises both successes and setbacks within a coherent strategy. Investors, after all, are rarely unsettled by bad news itself; they are unsettled when it appears without explanation or connection to a plan.

At its most effective, reporting is not a data dump but a *curated communication*. The numbers matter, but so does the sequence in which they appear, the emphasis placed on particular metrics, and the linkage between financial and operational data. A well-constructed update does more than reflect the past period's performance—it shows how decisions taken align with longer-term goals, highlights the rationale behind trade-offs, and gives investors a clear sense of the company's direction. This is as much about cognitive design as it is about finance: arranging information so that it can be absorbed, interpreted, and acted upon without distortion.

One of the most common failures in investor communication is assuming that all stakeholders share the same baseline understanding of the business. In reality, investors vary in familiarity with the industry, the product, and even basic operational terminology. The founder's role is to reduce cognitive friction by providing a consistent framework for reporting. This means establishing a core set of metrics that appear in every update, defined clearly and tracked over time. When metrics are changed, added, or retired, the decision should be explained to prevent the perception that they are being manipulated to tell a more favourable story. Consistency is the foundation upon which trust is built.

Equally important is the ability to *layer information*. Not all investors need or want the same level of detail, but the reporting architecture should allow for both high-level oversight and deeper analysis. This might take the form of a top-level executive summary, followed by operational detail for those who wish to drill down. The key is to make the path from summary to detail seamless, ensuring that anyone who questions a headline figure can find the supporting data quickly. This layered approach not only accommodates different preferences but also reduces the likelihood of misunderstandings escalating into disputes.

Pre-empting difficult conversations begins with anticipating the questions investors are likely to ask—and answering them before they are voiced. If customer acquisition cost has risen, the report should not simply state the figure; it should explain why it has risen, what corrective action is planned, and what impact it is expected to have on future growth. If a key hire has departed, the update should place that event within the broader talent strategy. By embedding the rationale within the report itself, the founder controls the framing and prevents the vacuum in which speculation thrives. *Silence on an issue rarely buys time; it accelerates concern.*

The frequency of reporting is another element of architecture that shapes investor confidence. While contractual obligations might specify quarterly reports, smart founders supplement these with more frequent, lighter-touch updates. These interim communications can be as simple as a monthly performance snapshot or a note on a major product milestone. They serve two purposes: first, they keep investors engaged in real time, making them more likely to provide timely support when needed; second, they reduce the tension that can build between formal reporting cycles, when silence is often interpreted as bad news.

Yet, structure alone is not enough. Tone matters. Investors are attuned to signals beyond the content of the report—the language used, the balance between optimism and realism, and the willingness to acknowledge uncertainty. An update that reads like a marketing brochure erodes credibility; one that reads like a post-mortem saps confidence. The goal is to project measured confidence: to convey that challenges are recognised, addressed, and integrated into the strategic plan. This balance reassures investors that the founder is neither in denial nor in despair, but operating with clear-eyed pragmatism.

Technology has changed the mechanics of reporting, but not its underlying principles. Modern dashboards, real-time analytics, and collaborative investor portals can make information more accessible, but they also increase the risk of overexposure. Providing 24/7 access to raw data without context invites misinterpretation. The founder's responsibility is to mediate between data abundance and strategic relevance, ensuring that technology serves the narrative rather than overwhelming it. Tools are valuable only when they reinforce disciplined communication, not when they replace it.

A final but often overlooked aspect of information architecture is the treatment of forward-looking statements. Projections are inherently uncertain, but the way they are presented can significantly influence investor expectations. Overly conservative forecasts may protect against disappointment but can dampen enthusiasm; overly aggressive ones can fuel short-term excitement at the cost of long-term credibility. The discipline here lies in grounding projections in clearly stated assumptions and linking them directly to operational levers. When assumptions change—as they inevitably will—the report should explain how those changes affect the forecast, reinforcing the perception that the company is steering with precision, not drifting with the current.

In sum, the architecture of reporting is not a back-office function—it is a core leadership skill. It demands a founder's attention not only to the accuracy of the data but to the psychology of those receiving it. Done well, it transforms reporting from a transactional obligation into a strategic asset, one that strengthens trust, aligns expectations, and reduces the risk of adversarial conversations. Investors will forgive missed targets more readily than they will forgive feeling misled or left in the dark. The founder who understands this will treat every report as an opportunity to build confidence, not simply as a document to be delivered.

Turning Investors into Advocates: Tactics for leveraging investors' networks, expertise, and influence without ceding control

An investor who simply provides capital is a financier. An investor who becomes a genuine advocate can be an accelerant to growth that no marketing spend or hiring spree can replicate. The distinction lies not in the size of the cheque but in the nature of the relationship. An advocate does not merely watch the company from the sidelines—they open doors, shape opportunities, and, crucially, lend their credibility to the founder's vision. The most successful founders are those who can tap this reservoir of value without inviting the risk of investors overstepping into operational decision-making. *It is a delicate balance: maximising the benefits of proximity without surrendering the autonomy to steer the business.*

Turning an investor into an advocate begins with recognising that advocacy is built on trust and mutual benefit, not on obligation. Too many founders assume that because an investor has a stake in the business, they will automatically champion it in their networks. In reality, advocacy requires alignment—investors must not only believe in the company's potential but also feel confident that lending their reputation to it strengthens rather than exposes them. This means that before asking for introductions or public endorsements, a founder must first establish a track record of delivering on commitments, maintaining transparent communication, and demonstrating consistent strategic judgment.

The strategic use of an investor's network is one of the most potent, and potentially dangerous, forms of leverage available to a founder. On the positive side, a single introduction can shortcut months of business development effort, secure a meeting with a difficult-to-access decision-maker, or attract top-tier talent. But the wrong introduction, made prematurely or without adequate context, can damage credibility in markets where first impressions are rarely reversible. The founder's responsibility is to be surgical in their requests: specifying the type of contact needed, articulating why that connection is strategically important, and equipping the investor with a concise, compelling narrative to share. *The more prepared the founder is, the more confidently the investor can act as an advocate.*

Expertise is another underutilised asset in the investor relationship. While many investors position themselves as strategic partners, the reality is that their value is often situational rather than universal. Some may excel at pricing strategy, others at regulatory navigation, others still at crisis management. The founder who understands the specific areas in which an investor can contribute meaningfully will make targeted asks that respect their time and expertise. This approach does two things: it increases the likelihood of getting high-quality input and it signals to the investor that the founder has the discernment to distinguish between when to seek guidance and when to rely on internal judgment.

The danger lies in allowing this input to blur into influence over operational control. Investors, particularly those with sector experience, may feel justified in pushing for their preferred strategic choices. It is here that boundaries must be drawn—not through confrontation, but through disciplined governance. By framing input as advisory rather than directive, and by ensuring that decision-making authority remains firmly within the company's leadership, the founder can accept valuable contributions without diluting their authority. One effective method is to establish formal channels for advice—scheduled strategy reviews, thematic workshops, or working groups—rather than allowing ad-hoc interventions to shape the agenda.

Advocacy is also about timing. An investor's influence can be most effective at key inflection points: a major fundraising round, an international market entry, or a high-stakes recruitment effort. A founder who hoards investor goodwill and deploys it sparingly will often extract more value than one who makes constant, low-priority requests. This selective approach also creates a sense of significance around each ask, making investors more likely to prioritise it and lend their full weight to the effort. The psychology is straightforward: when an investor sees that their involvement is reserved for moments of real consequence, they are more likely to view themselves as a trusted ally rather than an overused resource.

Public advocacy—whether through speaking engagements, media appearances, or industry events—can amplify a company's credibility far beyond its current scale. Having an investor with a respected personal brand publicly endorse the company can reposition it in the eyes of customers, partners, and even future investors. But public advocacy carries risks: it can set expectations higher than the company is ready to meet, or tie its reputation too closely to a single narrative that may evolve. Founders must ensure that the message aligns with the company's current reality and trajectory, and that both parties agree on how the business should be represented.

At its highest level, investor advocacy extends beyond individual opportunities and becomes a form of reputational stewardship. An investor with deep industry ties can subtly influence the narrative around a company in private conversations, shaping how other stakeholders perceive its trajectory. This form of advocacy is rarely visible to the founder but can be decisive in moments when confidence is fragile—during market downturns, leadership transitions, or periods of strategic uncertainty. Maintaining the conditions for this behind-the-scenes advocacy requires continuous relationship cultivation, not just when capital is being raised or when a favour is needed.

The thread that runs through all of this is reciprocity. Advocacy thrives when investors feel they are also receiving value beyond the financial return. This might mean offering them early insight into new product developments, involving them in thought-leadership initiatives, or connecting them with other founders in the portfolio who could benefit from their experience. The aim is to make the relationship feel like a two-way exchange rather than a series of one-sided requests. *An investor who sees themselves as an integral part of the company's success story will often work harder to ensure that story ends well.*

Ultimately, turning investors into advocates is less about persuasion than about creating the conditions in which advocacy is the natural, logical choice for them. It requires strategic clarity, disciplined boundaries, and a commitment to making each interaction count. When executed well, it transforms the investor-founder relationship from transactional to symbiotic—unlocking value that no term sheet can quantify, and doing so without ever surrendering the founder's control over the company's direction.

Navigating Conflict with Composure: Strategies for resolving disputes without damaging trust or long-term collaboration

In high-stakes business relationships, conflict is not a sign of failure but of engagement. Investors who never challenge decisions may either be disengaged or unaware of emerging risks. Disagreement, when managed with skill, can lead to stronger strategies and deeper mutual respect. But when handled poorly, even minor disputes can spiral into mistrust, disrupt operations, and cast long shadows over future collaboration. The true test of leadership is not avoiding conflict altogether but navigating it with a composure that safeguards both the immediate working relationship and the long-term alliance. *A founder's ability to remain centred under pressure often determines whether a dispute becomes a temporary tension or a permanent fracture.*

Composure in conflict begins well before any disagreement surfaces. It is rooted in the trust capital built through consistent, transparent communication during periods of alignment. When investors feel informed, valued, and respected in day-to-day interactions, they are more likely to assume good faith in moments of divergence. This is why the most effective founders treat every interaction as part of a cumulative trust ledger—one that can be drawn upon when difficult conversations arise. A strong relational foundation creates room for debate without it being interpreted as hostility.

In moments of conflict, emotional regulation becomes a strategic asset. A founder confronted with sharp criticism or aggressive questioning must resist the reflex to respond defensively or match the tone. Instead, active listening—genuinely hearing the investor's concerns without interruption—signals confidence and control. This does not mean passivity; it means allowing the other party to fully articulate their perspective before offering a considered response. In doing so, the founder often disarms the emotional charge of the moment, reframing the exchange as a search for solutions rather than a battle of wills.

Clarity of framing is critical. Disputes are rarely about the surface issue alone; they often reflect deeper concerns about risk appetite, growth pace, or strategic direction. A founder who can restate the conflict in terms of underlying principles rather than isolated incidents elevates the discussion. For instance, an argument over marketing spend might actually be about differing beliefs on capital efficiency in a tightening funding environment. By making the implicit explicit, the founder creates a platform for negotiation based on shared understanding rather than entrenched positions.

The language used in these moments matters enormously. Precision and neutrality reduce the risk of escalation, while inflammatory or absolute terms ("always," "never," "unacceptable") tend to harden opposition. Well-chosen phrasing—such as "I see the risk you're flagging" or "That's a perspective worth considering"—acknowledges the investor's stance without conceding prematurely. *Respect is conveyed not only through what is agreed but in how disagreement is handled.*

One of the most effective conflict resolution strategies is to separate the discussion of facts from the debate over interpretation. Agreeing on a common dataset—whether it is financial metrics, market research, or customer feedback—creates a factual anchor for the conversation. Once both parties are working from the same evidence, the dispute shifts from a contest of credibility to a genuine exchange of judgment. This not only improves the quality of the decision but reduces the temptation to turn the conflict into a referendum on competence.

It is also important to choose the right forum for resolution. Not all conflicts should be addressed in a board meeting or via group email. Sensitive disagreements often require a smaller, private setting where frankness can coexist with discretion. By managing the audience, the founder reduces the risk of public entrenchment—where participants defend their positions for the sake of appearance rather than substance. This approach protects reputations while keeping the door open for compromise.

Timing is another lever of composure. Some conflicts benefit from immediate attention to prevent them from festering; others require a cooling-off period to allow emotions to subside and facts to be gathered. The disciplined leader knows when to pause the discussion, framing the delay as an opportunity for reflection rather than avoidance. By signalling that the issue will be revisited at a specific time, the founder maintains momentum without rushing to resolution under suboptimal conditions.

In certain situations, involving a neutral third party—such as a respected industry advisor or an independent board member—can create space for a more balanced dialogue. This should not be framed as an escalation but as a way to broaden perspective and avoid stalemate. The third party's role is not to dictate an outcome but to ensure that both sides are heard fully and that the conversation remains anchored in shared objectives. The willingness to invite mediation demonstrates confidence and prioritisation of the relationship over ego.

While composure is often associated with calmness, it should not be mistaken for detachment. Passion for the company's mission can be expressed without letting it spill into hostility. The key is to ground passion in facts and strategic reasoning, making it a rallying point rather than a wedge. *When investors see that a founder's intensity is in service of the company's best interests rather than personal pride, they are more inclined to re-engage constructively.*

Over time, patterns of conflict resolution define the character of the founder-investor relationship. Consistently handling disputes with balance, transparency, and a focus on shared goals reinforces the perception that disagreements are part of a healthy governance process rather than warning signs of instability. It sets a tone where robust debate is welcomed, and where both parties can challenge each other without fear that the relationship will suffer lasting damage.

Ultimately, navigating conflict with composure is less about avoiding turbulence and more about becoming adept at steering through it. The founder who can face disagreement without defensiveness, who can distinguish between noise and signal, and who can emerge from disputes with relationships intact is not merely managing crises—they are shaping a culture of resilience and respect. In an environment where trust is the currency that underwrites every decision, this ability is not optional; it is the mark of enduring leadership.

Chapter 4
Milestones as Negotiation Tools

In the unpredictable world of high-growth entrepreneurship, milestones are too often reduced to simple checkboxes—a series of operational goals to be ticked off on the way to a distant vision. This perspective, however, is dangerously limited. For founders navigating capital markets, investor scrutiny, and the day-to-day pressures of scaling, milestones are far more than markers of progress: they are currency, leverage, and narrative anchors. They shape perception as much as they reflect achievement. When wielded strategically, milestones become instruments of influence, capable of swaying investor sentiment, unlocking favourable funding terms, buying critical time in moments of uncertainty, and cementing a leadership team's credibility when stakes run high. Understanding the difference between merely accomplishing a goal and framing that accomplishment to shift stakeholder dynamics can be the dividing line between survival and decline.

Adopting what might be termed the milestone mindset requires recognising that, in high-growth ventures, perception and progress are inseparable. Investors, strategic partners, and even core employees interpret milestones not solely as operational outputs, but as proxies for leadership, organisational health, and market traction. A product launch, a key customer win, or a revenue milestone carries weight beyond the numbers themselves; the impact depends on when it is delivered, to whom, and how it is contextualised. This is not about spin—it is about acknowledging that capital raising and strategic positioning are always entwined with perception. Founders who learn to craft, sequence, and communicate milestones with deliberate intent acquire a subtle but potent form of soft power that extends well beyond the figures on a balance sheet.

Yet even the most strategic deployment of milestones is constrained by a stark reality: resources are finite, and so too is investor patience. In most scaling ventures, the universe of potential targets outstrips the capacity to pursue them simultaneously. The critical question is not simply which goals to achieve, but which will yield the most strategic leverage at a given moment. This is where prioritisation under pressure becomes both art and discipline. Selecting the right milestones demands a careful calculus, balancing financial imperatives, market narratives, and operational readiness. Achieving a profitability target may signal resilience in a tightening funding environment, whereas securing a high-profile partnership might carry greater weight with strategic investors who prioritise long-term positioning over short-term margins. The sequencing of milestones—what comes first, what waits—shapes a company's capacity to retain negotiation power and preserve optionality.

Public and private wins further complicate the calculus. Some milestones are most effective when broadcast widely, shaping market perception, attracting investor attention, or signalling momentum to customers and partners. Others are better kept quiet, reserved for internal alignment or leveraged in private negotiations. Overexposure can dilute the impact of a genuinely transformative achievement; underexposure risks leaving stakeholders uncertain about progress. The decision to disclose—or withhold—is not a matter of marketing alone; it is a strategic choice that can recalibrate influence across the table. In competitive landscapes, revealing too much can invite aggressive moves from rivals or pressure from investors to accelerate scaling prematurely.

The power of this approach becomes clear in cases where milestone mastery changes a company's trajectory. Imagine a startup facing a funding gap, with its lead investor hesitant to commit. Rather than rush into a suboptimal deal, the founders focus scarce resources on delivering a single, high-impact milestone: securing a multi-year contract with a marquee client. When timed and communicated with precision, this achievement transforms the negotiation. Suddenly, the company is no longer a capital-constrained risk but a high-demand, strategically positioned player. This pivot enables the founders not only to secure the necessary funding but to negotiate improved terms and attract additional investors at an elevated valuation. Such outcomes are not rare accidents; they exemplify how thoughtfully chosen and framed milestones can reshape leverage entirely.

This chapter unpacks the milestone mindset in full. It challenges the notion that all progress is equal, showing why the selection, timing, and framing of achievements are inseparable from the politics of capital and growth. We explore decision-making frameworks that help founders prioritise which targets matter most at any given moment, recognising the inherent trade-offs. We examine the subtle but critical differences between milestones designed for public visibility and those reserved for private strategic influence. Throughout, the principles are illustrated by the lived experiences of founders who have converted moments of acute risk into strategic advantage—not by doing more, but by doing the right things, in the right order, and communicating them judiciously.

For founders who see milestones as instruments rather than mere metrics, negotiation strength is neither accidental nor transactional; it is the product of deliberate, evidence-informed choices. Operational execution is necessary, but insufficient on its own. The discipline lies in strategic storytelling, precise timing, and calibrated influence. The stakes are high, but so too is the reward when milestones evolve from simple markers of progress into levers of real power.

The Milestone Mindset: Why hitting (and framing) milestones is both a performance metric and a political tool

Milestones are often mistaken for neutral measurements of progress, as if they were objective waypoints on a company's journey, immune to interpretation. This belief is not only naïve—it can be strategically dangerous. In the context of capital-raising, strategic partnerships, and market positioning, milestones are rarely just about what has been achieved. They are also about *how* the achievement is framed, *when* it is revealed, and *who* is positioned to interpret it. A milestone is simultaneously a performance metric and a political signal. It operates in two domains: the operational reality of what has been accomplished, and the narrative reality of what stakeholders believe it means. Mastery comes from recognising that both matter equally.

In high-growth ventures, perception often moves as much capital as performance. A revenue target achieved ahead of schedule might reassure existing investors, but if framed poorly it could also trigger questions about why growth projections were conservative in the first place. Conversely, a milestone reached slightly late can still strengthen negotiating power if the surrounding story—about overcoming structural barriers, securing unexpected advantages, or achieving qualitative gains beyond the metric—is persuasive and credible. *The narrative context can, in some cases, outweigh the raw fact of the milestone itself.* This is why the most adept founders do not treat milestone communication as an afterthought. They engineer the sequence, timing, and framing with the same intentionality they bring to product launches or funding pitches.

The political dimension becomes most apparent in moments of high-stakes negotiation. Investors, board members, and potential acquirers often interpret milestones as predictive signals: indicators of whether a leadership team can deliver on its promises and manage resources effectively. This predictive element means milestones influence future confidence as much as they reflect past achievement. Consider the difference between telling a prospective investor that the company has "secured 50 enterprise clients" versus that it has "closed fifty multi-year enterprise contracts in a single quarter, double the prior period, while maintaining 92% gross margin." The latter is not only a stronger operational fact—it communicates a mastery of momentum, market positioning, and efficiency. It reframes the milestone from being a static number into being evidence of strategic competence.

The milestone mindset also demands an understanding that not all wins should be treated equally in public and private spheres. Some are better held back, shared selectively with specific stakeholders to gain leverage in targeted negotiations. Others need to be amplified to the market to shift perception at scale. For example, announcing a small but strategically critical regulatory approval might not move public sentiment much but could be decisive in talks with a single key investor or acquisition partner. On the other hand, trumpeting such an approval too early could embolden competitors or invite premature scrutiny. Timing, therefore, is not a secondary concern—it is central to maximising the strategic value of an achievement.

The framing of milestones is not manipulation; it is the discipline of ensuring that facts are contextualised in a way that serves the company's strategic objectives. In reality, every stakeholder applies their own frame to a milestone. Investors weigh it against portfolio performance and macroeconomic trends. Employees filter it through their sense of job security and career prospects. Customers assess it based on trust and market alternatives. If the leadership team does not actively shape the interpretation, it will be shaped for them—often in ways that dilute or distort the intended impact. *Control over milestone narrative is, in effect, a form of control over the company's perceived trajectory.*

Historical examples illustrate how the same milestone can be perceived in radically different ways. When Tesla announced reaching 5,000 Model 3 cars per week, some investors saw it as proof of scalability; others, aware of production line reconfigurations, viewed it as a temporary spike. The difference lay less in the number itself and more in the surrounding story—was it framed as the beginning of sustained high-volume manufacturing, or as the crest of an unsustainable push? Similarly, when a software startup announces crossing 1 million users, that number is impressive only if stakeholders believe those users are engaged, paying, and growing in value. Without a narrative that addresses retention, monetisation, and competitive positioning, the milestone risks being dismissed as vanity.

One of the less discussed but equally important aspects of the milestone mindset is *sequencing*. Achievements do not exist in isolation; their order creates a storyline that investors, partners, and markets interpret subconsciously. A strategic partnership signed before a major product release tells a different story than one announced afterwards. The first scenario suggests market validation and strategic foresight; the second implies endorsement following proof of product viability. Both are valuable, but they shape negotiations differently. Sequencing is about creating a chain of causality that reinforces the perception of momentum and inevitability—a perception that strengthens negotiating positions.

It is also essential to recognise that milestones are double-edged. The same achievement that strengthens credibility with one group can create unwanted pressure with another. A rapid spike in revenue growth might excite investors hungry for market dominance but alarm operational teams concerned about infrastructure strain. A major funding round, framed as validation, might simultaneously raise expectations to a level that leaves little room for iteration or course correction. The milestone mindset involves anticipating these tensions in advance and managing both the upside and downside narratives.

The most sophisticated operators integrate milestone strategy into the broader rhythm of corporate governance. They design board updates, investor communications, and public announcements with deliberate layering: immediate tactical wins are linked to medium-term strategic objectives, which in turn are tied to the company's overarching vision. This creates a coherence that reassures stakeholders and limits the risk of single achievements being misinterpreted as isolated events. By embedding each milestone within a larger arc, founders create resilience in their story—if one metric slips, the narrative of progress remains intact.

Ultimately, the milestone mindset is about moving from passive achievement to active leverage. It demands that leaders see each significant accomplishment not as the end of an effort but as the beginning of an opportunity to shape perception, influence negotiations, and solidify strategic advantage. In high-stakes environments, the difference between a company that merely hits its targets and one that uses those targets to redefine the conversation can be the difference between playing for survival and playing for dominance.

The leaders who internalise this approach operate with a different cadence. They do not simply report on milestones—they *deploy* them. They recognise that every achievement is both proof of competence and a political asset. And they understand that in a competitive, capital-driven world, it is not only the fact of progress that matters, but the skill with which that progress is turned into power.

Prioritisation Under Pressure: How to choose which goals to hit first when resources and investor patience are limited

When capital is finite and investor tolerance for delay is thin, prioritisation becomes a form of survival strategy. In such conditions, the challenge is not simply deciding what matters, but identifying which specific objectives—out of many competing possibilities—will generate the highest return on both financial and political capital. The wrong choice can deplete resources without shifting the company's position meaningfully; the right choice can create the momentum and credibility to unlock further time, funding, and trust. In high-pressure environments, *what you choose to do first is as much a statement of leadership as it is a tactical decision.*

Prioritisation under constraint is often wrongly framed as a purely operational problem—one to be solved with a checklist or a task-ranking matrix. In reality, it is a multi-dimensional judgment call, requiring the founder to balance immediate financial necessity, long-term strategic trajectory, and the complex psychology of stakeholder expectations. This means that the most effective prioritisation decisions are rarely about attacking the biggest problem or the largest market opportunity first. They are about sequencing wins in a way that sustains both operational viability and investor confidence. *A good prioritisation decision strengthens the company's balance sheet; a great one strengthens its negotiating position.*

Consider a company facing three potential targets: securing a large enterprise client, completing a core product feature, and hitting a user acquisition milestone that would trigger a funding release from an investor. All three have value, but they cannot all be achieved at once. The obvious temptation is to focus on whichever looks largest on paper—perhaps the enterprise client deal. Yet, if that deal would take six months to close and requires features still under development, it may be strategically unwise to prioritise it over the user acquisition milestone, which could unlock immediate funds and buy the time needed to close the deal later. The logic here is not about ignoring the big win, but staging wins so that each one extends the company's operational runway and strengthens its leverage for the next.

This sequencing logic becomes even more critical when investor patience is wearing thin. Stakeholders rarely view all goals as equally important; their perception of urgency is shaped by their own priorities, which may differ from the company's. Some investors are most concerned with revenue growth, others with proof of product-market fit, and others still with clear market leadership signals. *Choosing the right milestone to hit first often means aligning your definition of "urgent" with the urgency your most influential stakeholders feel.* Misalignment here can be costly—not just in terms of delayed funding, but in the erosion of trust and perceived competence.

The tension is that the goal most important to investors may not be the same as the goal most critical to the company's long-term sustainability. This is where disciplined prioritisation requires a dual-lens approach. The first lens asks: *Which goal, if achieved next, buys us the most breathing room?* The second lens asks: *Which goal, if achieved next, strengthens our ability to negotiate from a position of strength later?* The best choice under pressure is rarely a perfect overlap of these two, but the optimal move sits at the intersection of short-term necessity and long-term leverage.

There is also a psychological element to consider: early wins in a pressure environment have a disproportionate impact on morale, both internally and externally. Teams under strain need visible proof that progress is possible; investors need confirmation that their capital is working. A founder who prioritises an achievable but strategically meaningful target can re-energise their team, reduce investor anxiety, and shift the tone of future conversations. In this sense, prioritisation is not only about operational order but also about mood management—controlling the emotional narrative within the company and among its stakeholders.

Historical examples show that under high-pressure conditions, the most successful leaders have often favoured momentum-generating goals over grand but slow-burn objectives. Amazon, during its early growth phases, prioritised customer acquisition and revenue visibility metrics that reassured investors of market dominance before pursuing more complex logistical innovations. This was not because logistics were unimportant, but because hitting visible, investor-valued milestones bought the company the time and capital to make the deeper operational moves later.

Of course, prioritisation under pressure carries inherent risks. By focusing narrowly on investor-visible wins, a company can neglect foundational work that will be necessary later, creating future bottlenecks. The counterbalance to this risk is disciplined resource allocation—ensuring that even while the primary push is toward the politically and financially valuable milestone, a baseline of progress is maintained in other critical areas. This prevents the company from arriving at its next milestone with glaring weaknesses that undermine its negotiating position.

In situations of acute constraint, it can also be tempting to prioritise based solely on speed to completion. While speed matters, it is not a standalone justification. A fast win that is low in strategic or political value can consume resources and stakeholder attention without moving the needle. The discipline lies in filtering every potential goal through a simple but demanding question: *If we achieve this next, does it materially improve our position to secure the resources or market position we need?* If the answer is not a clear yes, it is a distraction.

The ability to make such decisions well often hinges on the founder's clarity of vision and willingness to communicate trade-offs transparently. Investors will tolerate, and even respect, a decision to deprioritise their preferred goal if they believe it is part of a coherent and credible sequence. This requires confidence, precision, and a track record of delivering on the sequence already in play. A founder who can articulate not just *what* they are prioritising, but *why this order matters*, earns the kind of trust that makes future prioritisation debates easier to navigate.

Ultimately, prioritisation under pressure is not about perfect optimisation—it is about sequencing high-value wins to sustain survival, create momentum, and shape the company's narrative in the eyes of those whose confidence determines its future. It is an exercise in both operational logic and political intelligence, demanding that leaders weigh not only what advances the business mechanically, but also what strengthens their influence in the high-stakes theatre of growth. Those who master it understand that the first goal you hit under constraint is never just a metric—it is the opening move in the negotiation for your company's next chapter.

Public vs. Private Wins: When to trumpet achievements for market perception and when to keep progress internal

Not every victory should be paraded in the public square. In the life of a growing company, the decision to publicise an achievement or to keep it within the walls of the boardroom is not simply a matter of communications preference—it is a strategic choice with real consequences for investor confidence, competitor behaviour, employee morale, and market positioning. *The visibility of a win can be as consequential as the win itself.* Managing that visibility is therefore a core leadership skill, and it demands as much judgment as deciding which milestones to pursue in the first place.

The urge to announce progress is understandable. Start-ups and scaling companies live in an attention economy where investor enthusiasm, talent attraction, and customer confidence can be fuelled by well-timed news. Publicly trumpeting a win—a major contract signed, a funding round closed, a product launched—can create an upward narrative that makes subsequent achievements easier to secure. Capital flows more readily towards perceived momentum; prospective hires are more willing to gamble on a company that looks like it is on the rise. In this sense, public wins are not just communications—they are instruments for amplifying credibility and opportunity.

But the same announcement that excites stakeholders can also alert competitors, set expectations unrealistically high, or shift bargaining dynamics against the company. Publicising the signing of a major enterprise client, for example, may attract rivals' attention before the relationship has been cemented operationally, inviting poaching attempts or competitive counter-offers. It can also lead other prospective clients to assume your pricing is inflexible or that your delivery capacity is already at maximum strain. *Every public win is also an information leak*, and the strategic cost of that leak must be weighed against the potential reputational benefit.

There is also a temporal dimension to consider. The value of a public announcement is not fixed; it depends on timing, context, and sequencing. Announcing a major technological breakthrough six months before it can be commercially deployed may generate buzz but also risk fatigue or scepticism when revenue does not materialise quickly. By contrast, holding that announcement until there is a clear path to monetisation can transform the same piece of news from speculative excitement into compelling evidence of execution. In markets where attention spans are short and cycles of enthusiasm volatile, the discipline to delay an announcement until its impact can be maximised is a competitive advantage in itself.

Private wins—those achievements deliberately kept internal—serve a different but equally important strategic purpose. They allow a company to consolidate gains without external scrutiny, to prepare for the next stage without the distortion of outside expectations, and to avoid signalling to competitors where its strategic bets are being placed. Internalising certain milestones can also give leadership greater control over narrative pacing; rather than being dragged by the calendar of news cycles, they can choose the moment when a cluster of achievements can be unveiled together for maximum effect.

This is particularly relevant when dealing with investors. While public announcements can reassure them of progress, there is a category of investor-sensitive wins that may be better managed privately until they are ready to withstand public market or media interpretation. For example, achieving a critical manufacturing efficiency that significantly improves margins may be highly valuable for investor confidence but might be more potent if revealed alongside broader operational improvements rather than as an isolated fact. In private settings, such information can deepen investor trust without broadcasting it to competitors or creating pressures that distort strategic flexibility.

The decision between public and private is rarely binary. There is often a hybrid approach: selectively disclosing certain elements of an achievement while keeping others under wraps. A company might announce that it has expanded into a new market without naming the flagship customer that made the expansion viable. Or it might share broad performance metrics without revealing the specific product features or operational changes driving those numbers. This allows the company to enjoy the reputational benefits of progress while protecting the strategic levers that underpin it.

Founders must also be aware of the psychological effects of publicising wins internally versus externally. Public wins energise employees by showing that the outside world recognises their efforts; they validate the hard work and can boost morale in ways internal memos cannot. Yet, too many public announcements, especially if they are overhyped, can create internal cynicism when the gap between public perception and internal reality grows too wide. Private wins, on the other hand, can foster a sense of disciplined focus within the team—a shared understanding that not all victories need to be celebrated externally to matter deeply.

The most skilful operators use the visibility of wins to manage relationships with different audiences. With the press and the broader market, they choose announcements that enhance positioning without exposing vulnerabilities. With investors, they may reveal more detail privately to maintain credibility and support ongoing funding needs. With employees, they might share certain internal wins early to sustain morale, even if those wins will not be public for months. *The same achievement can be packaged differently for each audience, depending on the intended effect.*

One telling example comes from the SaaS sector. A mid-stage software company landed a transformative partnership with a Fortune 500 firm. The temptation to announce it immediately was immense; the logo alone would elevate the company's standing. But the CEO chose to keep it private for six months while the partnership was operationally embedded. During this period, the team quietly adapted infrastructure to handle the anticipated demand, locked in related customer contracts, and negotiated more favourable financing terms using the partnership as leverage in confidential investor discussions. When the deal was finally announced, it came packaged with evidence of successful execution and related growth metrics—transforming what would have been a speculative announcement into a multi-dimensional proof point.

Conversely, there are cases where delaying a public win can backfire. If a competitor releases similar news first, the impact of your own achievement can be diluted or even dismissed as a copycat move. In industries where perception of innovation leadership is critical—such as biotechnology, fintech, or consumer electronics—being second to announce can materially weaken strategic positioning. Here, the calculus shifts: it may be better to accept the risks of early disclosure than to forfeit first-mover narrative advantage.

In the end, the decision about when to trumpet and when to remain silent is a sophisticated balancing act. It requires a clear understanding of the company's strategic objectives, the dynamics of its competitive landscape, the psychology of its stakeholders, and the sequencing of its broader growth narrative. Public wins can build momentum, attract resources, and shape market perception in ways that private wins cannot. But private wins can protect competitive advantage, allow controlled execution, and keep the company's narrative grounded in reality rather than hype. The most effective leaders resist the reflex to broadcast every success; instead, they treat each potential announcement as a strategic asset, to be deployed at the right time, to the right audience, with the right framing to serve not just the moment but the long game.

Case Study: Milestones that Saved a Startup: Real-world example of milestone mastery averting a funding crisis

In early 2019, a London-based healthtech start-up, VitalTrack, found itself in the kind of precarious financial position that kills more companies than competition ever will. On paper, the business had everything going for it: a patent-pending wearable device capable of real-time monitoring for chronic heart conditions, a small but talented engineering team, and a handful of early clinical partnerships. Yet beneath the promising veneer, its bank balance had less than five months of runway left, an ongoing Series A process had stalled, and investor patience was wearing dangerously thin. The founders were staring down a fundamental reality: unless they could present unequivocal proof of market traction, their next round would not close in time.

The problem wasn't that VitalTrack had been idle. They had made progress on several fronts—refining their algorithms, improving manufacturing tolerances, and securing regulatory clearance for their device in the UK. But these achievements were either invisible to most investors or too technical to serve as compelling, non-negotiable proof of commercial potential. Their pitch deck leaned heavily on the promise of future adoption rather than present, measurable success. *The gap between operational progress and externally recognisable milestones was the existential threat.*

The turning point came when the CEO reframed the company's approach from a laundry list of ongoing efforts to a focused sprint towards a single, high-impact milestone: a signed contract with a top-tier private hospital group, complete with a paid pilot deployment and patient outcome tracking. This was not a simple redirection—it required brutal prioritisation. R&D sprints were cut back, certain feature developments were postponed, and every available sales and operational resource was redirected towards winning and implementing that one deal. The founders understood that, in their specific crisis, *the most valuable currency was the perception of market adoption by credible customers.*

Crucially, they recognised that securing the contract was only part of the milestone's power. Framing it for maximum strategic leverage was equally important. It was not enough to say they had signed a customer—they needed to present it as the definitive evidence that their product had crossed the threshold from prototype to indispensable medical tool. Internally, the sales lead worked with the hospital's administration to fast-track integration into two departments rather than the originally planned single unit, creating a more impressive deployment story. The data science team worked nights to ensure that, within the first month, outcome data could be shared showing measurable reductions in hospital readmissions for high-risk cardiac patients.

When the announcement was made, it was carefully engineered. The company issued a joint press release with the hospital group, which carried more reputational weight than a self-published update. The story was pitched to trade media not just as a contract win but as part of a broader narrative about innovation in preventative care.

Simultaneously, in private investor briefings, they shared detailed early results from the pilot—numbers that, while not yet public, showed a statistically significant clinical benefit. This two-tiered communication strategy meant that public perception was buoyed by credible headlines while investors felt they had privileged access to even more promising, granular data.

The result was immediate. Two institutional investors who had been on the fence re-engaged within a fortnight, citing the deal as a clear signal that VitalTrack's market was ready. The Series A round closed six weeks later, oversubscribed by 30 per cent. The hospital contract itself brought in only a modest sum relative to the funding target, but its symbolic and narrative value was disproportionate. *It transformed the company's story from "innovative but unproven" to "adopted and scaling."*

There were, however, deeper strategic lessons in this episode beyond the surface narrative of "land a big client, save the company." First, the milestone's success lay in its specificity and measurability. The founders did not attempt to string together a mix of vague indicators like "positive early feedback" or "increased pipeline interest." They chose a concrete, externally verifiable outcome that spoke directly to investor concerns about adoption risk. In distressed funding situations, ambiguity kills; specificity reassures.

Second, the framing of the milestone mattered as much as the achievement itself. Without the hospital's brand association, without rapid generation of outcome data, and without careful sequencing of public and private disclosures, the same contract might have been perceived as a promising but isolated event. Instead, it was positioned as the first domino in a sequence of adoption wins, making it far easier for investors to imagine the scaling story.

Third, prioritisation was not just about focus—it was about trade-offs made in full view of their implications. Delaying certain R&D features was not risk-free; competitors could have used the breathing room to close the gap. But the leadership recognised that without immediate capital, those future features would never see the light of day. This level of decision-making discipline is often the hardest for founders who are emotionally invested in product roadmaps, yet it is essential when the company's very existence is on the line.

Finally, the case illustrated that a milestone's true impact often comes from the ecosystem it unlocks, not just the milestone itself. The hospital deployment led to inbound interest from other healthcare providers, which in turn created competitive tension among potential partners. It also generated patient testimonials that became marketing assets in their own right. By choosing a milestone that was both a proof point and a catalyst, VitalTrack created a self-reinforcing loop of credibility and opportunity.

For many founders, this kind of pivot under pressure feels counterintuitive. The instinct is to keep pushing forward on multiple fronts, hoping that cumulative progress will speak for itself. VitalTrack's experience shows that, in moments of existential risk, cumulative progress often lacks the clarity and narrative power that investors require. A single, undeniable, and well-framed milestone can do more to secure survival than a dozen diffuse indicators of momentum.

By the end of 2020, VitalTrack had expanded its deployments to five hospital groups, secured partnerships in two international markets, and had doubled its headcount with the capital raised. Yet inside the leadership team, the memory of that early 2019 scramble remained vivid—not as a cautionary tale of crisis, but as the moment they learned the strategic art of milestone mastery. It was not luck that saved them, nor simply hard work, but *the deliberate choice of the right milestone, pursued with disciplined focus and framed for maximum impact.* In the unforgiving arithmetic of start-up survival, that choice was worth more than any feature, prototype, or marketing campaign they could have produced in the same period.

Chapter 5
Scaling Without Implosion

The moments following a significant funding round carry a heady mixture of relief, pride, and ambition. For founders who have endured years of risk, sleepless nights, and financial scrimping, seeing the bank account flush with capital can feel like vindication. Teams are invigorated, previously distant growth plans seem suddenly within reach, and the air is thick with possibility. Yet, precisely in this euphoric state, the seeds of instability are often planted. Capital, while a powerful enabler, is also an amplifier: it magnifies strengths, but it magnifies weaknesses even more. In the hands of a leadership team unprepared for the complexities of rapid scaling, money can accelerate fragility as quickly as it accelerates growth.

Overexpansion rarely manifests as a single catastrophic error. More often, it emerges through a sequence of rational, well-intentioned choices: opening a new sales office to "capture additional demand", launching multiple product lines to "diversify risk", or doubling headcount to "match projected growth". Each action can make sense in isolation, but without a solid foundation, the cumulative effect is perilous. Founders frequently mistake post-funding momentum for structural capacity, overlooking that growth—whether in revenue, team size, or geographic footprint—brings entirely new operational demands. Systems that served a 20-person company in one market often fracture under the weight of a 100-person team spanning multiple regions. The peril lies not only in moving fast, but in stretching an organisational framework beyond its design limits.

This is why the first discipline of responsible scaling is preparation, not acceleration. Before chasing growth, founders must examine whether their organisational and technical infrastructure can sustain the pressures they intend to apply. This encompasses customer onboarding processes, support systems, financial controls capable of handling complexity, and leadership bandwidth to maintain alignment across a swelling team. Underdeveloped infrastructure does more than slow growth; it spawns operational chaos, drains management focus, erodes customer trust, and distracts from strategic priorities. Companies that scale effectively invest in fortifying these internal systems before extending their external reach.

Yet infrastructure is only part of the story; people matter just as much. Scaling tests culture in ways that no other stage can. Rapid recruitment, particularly under pressure, can dilute the values and behaviours that initially made the team effective. Early hires often bonded through shared sacrifice and a unifying mission, while new employees—especially those arriving from larger organisations—may bring different instincts and tolerance for risk. Founders who neglect to consciously preserve and adapt cultural foundations during expansion often discover, too late, that trust, cohesion, and shared purpose have frayed. Culture is not merely a set of rituals; it is the glue that prevents operational speed from deteriorating into organisational drift.

Managing this cultural dimension requires constant vigilance. Revenue growth alone does not guarantee organisational health; fissures in trust, communication, and morale can quietly accumulate and undermine performance. Leaders must monitor these tensions not only through formal surveys or metrics but also through active presence and listening. Preserving core values is not about resisting change—it is about distinguishing which aspects of culture are immutable and which can evolve without compromising identity.

Resilient scaling strategies are often selective and asymmetric. Rather than pursuing across-the-board expansion, founders can achieve more sustainable results by scaling strategically at the edges—targeted areas that amplify the broader organisation. This might involve strengthening customer success before ramping acquisition, or establishing a robust operations team in a single high-potential region before pursuing global reach. Such measured steps may lack immediate spectacle, but they maintain flexibility and protect the company from destabilising shocks.

Ultimately, scaling is less a binary choice between boldness and caution than a disciplined exercise in timing, sequencing, and calibration. Successful founders orchestrate growth in ways that preserve operational stability and strategic optionality. They recognise early warning signs of overreach, prepare the organisation to bear increased load before applying pressure, and design expansion strategies that safeguard both cultural and structural integrity. Contrary to the popular mantra of "move fast and break things," rebuilding trust, systems, and culture after an implosion is far costlier than building them correctly from the outset.

In the chapters ahead, we will explore the mechanisms that keep growth from tipping into chaos: identifying early signals of overexpansion, constructing systems and leadership capacity to sustain scaling, protecting cultural cohesion amidst rapid hiring, and deploying targeted growth strategies that extend capability without destabilising foundations. By treating expansion as a deliberate, managed process rather than a frenetic dash, founders can ensure that their companies do not merely grow bigger, but grow stronger. Ambition remains essential, but it must be channelled through structures capable of bearing its weight over the long term.

The Temptation of Overexpansion: Why founders often overreach post-funding and how to recognise the warning signs

The most dangerous moment in a company's growth arc is not always when it is fighting for survival; often it is when it is flush with capital. The injection of a significant funding round can shift a founder's psychology from scarcity to abundance almost overnight. Strategies that were once carefully paced are suddenly compressed into aggressive timelines, and initiatives that were once rigorously scrutinised for return on investment are pursued simply because they are now financially feasible. This abundance of resources can distort decision-making, blurring the line between strategic opportunity and reckless ambition. The problem is not ambition itself—it is ambition unmoored from operational capacity, market readiness, and disciplined prioritisation. When money arrives faster than maturity, the temptation to overexpand becomes not just a risk but an inevitability for many.

Overexpansion is rarely the product of ignorance; it is often rooted in a founder's genuine desire to capitalise on momentum and satisfy investor expectations. Post-funding, there is an implicit—sometimes explicit—pressure to deliver rapid, visible growth. New board members want metrics to move in quarters, not years. Media coverage amplifies the narrative of an unstoppable rise. Early hires who endured lean years anticipate a more generous budget for projects, tools, and hires. This collective anticipation can push leadership to pursue multiple high-cost initiatives in parallel: international expansion, aggressive headcount growth, simultaneous product launches. In isolation, each of these moves might be defensible. Together, they can strain leadership bandwidth, dilute focus, and create fragility across every layer of the organisation.

One of the most common manifestations of overexpansion is geographical overreach. A company achieving strong traction in its home market often assumes that replicating this success in new regions is simply a matter of translating marketing materials and hiring local sales teams. In reality, each new market introduces layers of operational complexity—local regulations, cultural differences, logistical challenges—that can multiply unpredictably. The assumption that success in one market guarantees success in another is a classic scaling fallacy. What's more, expanding into multiple new markets simultaneously increases the chance that leadership attention is spread too thin to address early signs of trouble in any one of them.

Another high-risk form of overexpansion is product proliferation. Flush with capital, founders may accelerate secondary product lines or entirely new offerings before their flagship product has reached maturity. While diversification can be a sound long-term strategy, premature expansion often results in half-built products competing for resources with the core offering. This can slow the refinement of the primary revenue driver, weaken market positioning, and erode brand clarity. A company known for doing one thing exceptionally well can quickly become a company known for doing many things to a mediocre standard. In the short term, this may not immediately harm topline growth; in the long term, it can erode the trust and loyalty that underpin sustainable market leadership.

Headcount growth is perhaps the most seductive and the most deceptive form of overexpansion. Large funding rounds almost always lead to rapid hiring, partly because talent acquisition is viewed as an investment in future capacity, and partly because an influx of people signals growth to investors and the market. The challenge lies in the lag between hiring and productivity. New employees take time to onboard, integrate into culture, and begin contributing at full capacity. If hiring runs ahead of operational readiness—clear processes, defined roles, leadership bandwidth—the company can find itself with inflated payroll costs and reduced organisational efficiency. Ironically, instead of accelerating growth, overhiring can slow it, as managers spend disproportionate time resolving misalignments and friction among teams.

Founders often underestimate how quickly complexity compounds during overexpansion. Each new office, product, or hire adds not just incremental cost but also coordination demands, communication channels, and decision-making layers. What once could be managed with informal check-ins now requires formal reporting structures and governance. Without a deliberate investment in these operational scaffolds, the quality of decision-making erodes. Leaders begin to operate reactively rather than strategically, constantly firefighting the unintended consequences of their own rapid expansion.

Recognising the warning signs of overexpansion requires disciplined self-awareness and a willingness to interrogate whether growth is being pursued because it is strategically sound or simply because it is financially possible. Among the earliest indicators are declining quality metrics—customer satisfaction scores slipping, product bugs increasing, project timelines slipping—paired with an uptick in internal friction. Another signal is leadership fatigue: when executives find themselves spending most of their time troubleshooting rather than driving strategic initiatives, it suggests that the organisation's growth has outpaced its ability to self-manage. Financially, cash burn rates accelerating faster than planned, without a proportionate improvement in key performance indicators, should trigger immediate scrutiny.

Importantly, the presence of capital does not make these risks less relevant—it magnifies them. Abundant resources can mask underlying inefficiencies for a time, making it harder to see that the organisation is structurally overextended until it faces a market downturn, an investor pullback, or an operational crisis. Founders must resist the cognitive bias that equates available capital with readiness to scale. The discipline is to evaluate each potential expansion move against three filters: operational capacity, market readiness, and cultural resilience. If even one of these is underdeveloped, the risk of destabilisation increases exponentially.

Some of the most enduring companies take a counterintuitive approach in the immediate aftermath of a major funding event: they slow down. This is not inertia; it is calibration. They use the new capital to strengthen their core—refining product-market fit, building robust operational systems, deepening customer relationships—before layering on complex expansion initiatives. This patience is difficult to maintain under investor and market pressure, but it often distinguishes those who sustain long-term leadership from those who burn brightly and fade quickly. The reality is that overexpansion is not merely a tactical misstep—it is a strategic misalignment between resources and readiness. Founders who understand this treat capital as a catalyst for disciplined, staged growth rather than an excuse to accelerate in all directions at once.

Ultimately, the temptation of overexpansion is a test of leadership maturity. It asks whether a founder can hold the tension between ambition and restraint, between seizing opportunity and preserving stability. The leaders who pass this test are those who view growth not as a sprint to be completed before the money runs out, but as a series of deliberate moves designed to build an organisation capable of thriving at the scale they envision. They know that the fastest way to implode a business is to give it more to manage than its systems, people, and culture can sustain. And they understand that the true art of scaling is not just about how far or fast you go, but about knowing exactly when not to move at all.

Infrastructure Before Acceleration: Building the systems, teams, and processes that can handle growth without chaos

The greatest irony in scaling is that the very capital meant to propel a company forward can, if deployed without preparation, become the catalyst for its unravelling. Growth is intoxicating, but it is also unforgiving. Without the structural foundations to support it, expansion magnifies every operational weakness, exposes cultural fissures, and forces leadership into perpetual firefighting. This is why disciplined founders understand that the real determinant of sustainable growth is not the size of their funding round, but the resilience and adaptability of the infrastructure they build before acceleration begins. Infrastructure, in this context, is not a vague metaphor—it is the tangible architecture of systems, processes, and teams that can maintain coherence and control in the face of scaling pressures.

In the early stages of a startup, flexibility is prized. Processes are often informal, roles fluid, and systems improvised. This agility is an asset when the team is small and the scope manageable, allowing for rapid pivots and opportunistic decision-making. Yet what serves a company well in its scrappy beginnings can become a liability at scale. As headcount grows, customer volumes increase, and product lines diversify, the absence of clearly defined processes leads to confusion, duplication of work, and costly delays. *Founders who mistake the survival-driven ingenuity of the early phase for a scalable operating model risk discovering too late that speed without structure is chaos in disguise.*

A robust scaling infrastructure is built on three interlocking pillars: operational systems, organisational capability, and governance. Operational systems include everything from IT architecture and data management protocols to supply chain logistics and customer service frameworks. These systems must be designed not for current demand but for anticipated scale, allowing the business to absorb growth without constant reinvention. Organisational capability refers to the skills, leadership, and cultural norms that enable teams to operate effectively in increasingly complex environments. Governance encompasses decision-making frameworks, accountability structures, and mechanisms for maintaining alignment across multiple functions and geographies. Without balance across these pillars, the load of growth will fall disproportionately on one, causing it to crack under pressure.

A common trap is underinvesting in systems because they are perceived as a drag on agility. Early-stage companies often defer implementing enterprise-grade tools, structured reporting, or documented workflows, reasoning that these can be introduced "once growth justifies the cost." The flaw in this thinking is that by the time growth makes the investment unavoidable, the organisation is already operating at a pace and complexity that makes retrofitting these systems far more expensive and disruptive. For example, migrating customer data into a scalable CRM is relatively simple when you have hundreds of clients; doing so when you have tens of thousands risks operational downtime, frustrated customers, and lost revenue. The lesson is clear: *infrastructure built in anticipation of scale is an enabler of speed, not an impediment to it.*

The human element of infrastructure is just as critical. Scaling is ultimately a people challenge disguised as a systems challenge. Teams that function well at 20 people often struggle at 200, not because the talent is inferior but because the modes of communication, trust-building, and conflict resolution that worked in a tight-knit group do not translate naturally to larger, more distributed structures. This is where intentional organisational design comes into play. Defining roles and responsibilities, creating leadership layers, and introducing mechanisms for cross-functional collaboration are essential steps in avoiding the drift towards siloed, disconnected operations. The quality of these structures determines whether growth generates momentum or entropy.

Real-world examples abound of companies that accelerated before their infrastructure was ready, with predictable consequences. A technology startup expanding rapidly across Europe and Asia underestimated the complexity of regional compliance regulations, resulting in costly legal disputes and delayed product launches. A fast-growing e-commerce platform doubled its order volume in six months but failed to scale its warehouse and logistics systems accordingly, leading to delivery backlogs and customer attrition. These were not failures of market opportunity—they were failures of infrastructure readiness. Conversely, companies that invest early in scalable systems, like Amazon's relentless focus on fulfilment capabilities long before they were profitable, create a competitive moat that makes future growth almost frictionless.

Building infrastructure before acceleration also requires recognising the limits of founder bandwidth. Many entrepreneurs underestimate the degree to which scaling requires them to transition from being hands-on operators to orchestrators of complex systems. The founder who insists on being the decision bottleneck in every strategic matter will slow the organisation to a crawl, no matter how advanced the systems. This is why leadership development and delegation are foundational to infrastructure. The team must be equipped and empowered to make high-quality decisions without constant founder intervention, supported by clear metrics, reporting lines, and feedback loops.

One of the most valuable practices in this preparatory phase is scenario planning. Instead of reacting to growth milestones as they happen, disciplined companies map potential inflection points in advance—doubling customer volumes, expanding into new territories, integrating an acquisition—and assess the infrastructure requirements each would demand. This allows them to invest in systems, talent, and processes ahead of the curve, reducing the risk of being blindsided by operational bottlenecks. Such foresight is particularly critical in volatile markets, where the pace of change can render reactive scaling strategies obsolete overnight.

The resistance to building infrastructure early is often rooted in cultural perception. In many startup circles, there is an implicit bias against processes, equating them with bureaucracy and stifled innovation. Yet in reality, well-designed systems *liberate* teams from operational friction, enabling them to focus more of their energy on creative problem-solving and value creation. The key is to build processes that are proportionate, adaptable, and aligned with company culture—not rigid frameworks imported wholesale from large corporations, but systems tailored to the unique rhythms and priorities of the business.

Ultimately, building infrastructure before acceleration is not about slowing growth; it is about ensuring that when growth comes, it is sustainable, profitable, and strategically aligned. It is the difference between a company that expands in controlled stages, consolidating each gain before moving to the next, and one that surges forward only to collapse under the weight of its own unmanaged complexity. The companies that endure are those that treat infrastructure not as an afterthought, but as the foundation on which all future acceleration rests. This is not the glamorous work that makes headlines—it is the quiet, deliberate investment that determines whether the headlines are about your meteoric rise or your spectacular implosion.

Culture Under Strain: How rapid hiring and structural changes affect team cohesion, and how to preserve your core values

One of the most underappreciated truths in business is that culture is not static—it is a living system that evolves with every new hire, every reorganisation, and every leadership decision. When a company scales rapidly, particularly after a major funding round, this system comes under intense pressure. The founder's vision, once carried instinctively by a small, tight-knit team, must now be transmitted through layers of people who did not share the early battles, the late nights, or the formative struggles. *The faster the headcount grows, the greater the risk that the original cultural DNA becomes diluted, distorted, or outright lost.* This is not simply a "soft" problem—it has tangible effects on performance, decision quality, and long-term sustainability.

Rapid hiring is often framed as a sign of momentum, a marker that the business is expanding successfully. In reality, each new hire introduces complexity. They arrive with their own professional norms, communication styles, and implicit expectations about how work should be done. In small doses, this diversity strengthens the organisation. But when dozens—or hundreds—of new people join in quick succession, the company's informal social agreements struggle to keep pace. Unspoken rules that once bound the early team together become unclear, leading to friction, misinterpretations, and the erosion of trust. Without conscious intervention, *culture doesn't scale by default—it fragments.*

Structural changes amplify this strain. As organisations grow, they naturally create new departments, layers of management, and reporting lines. This is necessary to maintain order, but it also alters the very fabric of how people interact. Teams that once collaborated directly may find themselves separated by hierarchies or physical distance. Decision-making becomes less about direct conversation and more about process, which—if not carefully designed—can feel bureaucratic and alienating. For employees who thrived in the intimacy of the startup phase, this shift can feel like a loss of identity and autonomy. For newer hires, it can create the impression that the company's values are slogans rather than lived realities.

The critical challenge is that these cultural shifts rarely announce themselves with clarity. Erosion happens incrementally—first a subtle decline in information sharing, then an increase in territorial thinking, then the quiet departure of early employees who no longer recognise the place they helped build. By the time the problem is acknowledged at the leadership level, the gap between the stated culture and the experienced culture may be wide enough to require an organisational rebuild. This is why *founders must treat cultural preservation as a parallel priority to revenue growth during scale-up phases, not as a secondary concern to be "fixed later."*

Preserving core values in the midst of rapid change begins with clarity. Vague aspirational statements like "we value innovation" or "we put customers first" are insufficient unless translated into observable behaviours that employees can model. If collaboration is a core value, leaders must define how it looks in practice—whether it means cross-department project ownership, shared accountability for results, or open-access communication channels. Without this specificity, new hires will default to the norms of their previous workplaces, unintentionally importing systems and behaviours that are misaligned with the company's identity.

Leadership modelling is equally critical. In moments of strain, employees look to leaders for cues about what truly matters. If executives bypass agreed processes in the name of speed, or reward outcomes at the expense of the behaviours that align with company values, the cultural signal is clear: the stated principles are negotiable. This is particularly dangerous during scale, when operational pressures are high and expediency is tempting. *Values survive structural change only if they are visible in leadership actions under pressure, not just in all-hands presentations when times are good.*

The hiring process itself is a frontline tool for cultural preservation. While speed is often the priority in aggressive growth phases, sacrificing cultural alignment for the sake of filling seats is one of the most expensive mistakes a scaling company can make. The cost is not just in recruitment churn—it's in the compounding effect of introducing behaviours that work against the company's operating rhythm. This is why the most disciplined scale-ups invest in structured cultural interviews, peer assessments, and onboarding processes that explicitly socialise new hires into the company's values before task expectations dominate.

Onboarding, in particular, is a make-or-break moment. In fast-growth environments, onboarding can become a perfunctory checklist, focused almost entirely on tools and procedures. Yet this is the period when a new employee is most impressionable—when their mental model of "how things are done here" is formed. If the onboarding process communicates the organisation's values through lived examples, stories from early days, and practical demonstrations of cultural norms, the likelihood of integration rises sharply. If it is purely transactional, new hires will shape their behaviour according to what they observe day-to-day, which may not align with the intended culture.

Maintaining cohesion under structural change also requires intentional bridge-building between old and new team members. Early employees hold institutional memory—an understanding of why the company made certain strategic decisions, how crises were navigated, and what trade-offs were accepted in pursuit of the mission. New employees bring fresh perspectives, skill sets, and industry practices. Left to chance, these groups can drift into "us versus them" dynamics, with early staff seeing newcomers as outsiders, and newcomers perceiving early staff as resistant to change. Leaders who consciously create mixed teams, joint problem-solving opportunities, and spaces for informal connection can turn this tension into a productive exchange rather than a fault line.

In distributed or hybrid work environments, cultural strain has an added dimension: physical separation. The absence of casual in-person interactions makes it harder for unspoken norms to be transmitted organically. Remote teams require deliberate cultural reinforcement—structured communication rhythms, digital rituals, and leadership visibility that compensate for the lack of spontaneous contact. Companies that fail to adapt their cultural practices to remote contexts risk developing multiple micro-cultures, each with its own unwritten rules, undermining cohesion further.

Finally, it is worth acknowledging that not every aspect of the early culture should be preserved. Some behaviours and norms that were effective in a team of ten can become liabilities in a team of one hundred. The aim is not to fossilise the culture but to distil and protect the elements that define the organisation's identity and competitive advantage, while allowing operational methods to evolve. This requires discernment: knowing which values are foundational and non-negotiable, and which are situational habits that can be adapted without losing the company's essence.

Culture under strain is not a side effect of scaling—it is an inevitable stage in the process. The difference between companies that emerge stronger and those that fracture lies in whether they treat culture as an asset to be actively managed, or as a background condition to be taken for granted. In the high-velocity environment of rapid hiring and structural change, preserving cohesion is neither sentimental nor symbolic—it is a strategic necessity that directly shapes the organisation's capacity to sustain growth without losing itself in the process.

Scaling at the Edges: Targeted growth strategies that expand capacity without destabilising the core business

One of the most dangerous misconceptions in business scaling is that growth must come from the centre—doubling down on existing operations, aggressively increasing output, and assuming that the infrastructure, people, and processes that worked yesterday will automatically stretch to meet tomorrow's demands. In reality, the healthiest, most sustainable expansions often take place at the edges of a business: small, deliberate extensions of capability, geography, or offering that increase reach without overwhelming the core. *Scaling at the edges is not about avoiding ambition; it is about ensuring ambition does not outpace the organisation's capacity to sustain itself.*

The allure of a centralised scaling push is understandable. The core of a business is where its identity, revenue, and operational mastery live. Pouring investment directly into these areas feels logical and controllable. Yet history is littered with examples of companies that broke themselves by forcing the core to grow faster than it could adapt. Manufacturing lines overwhelmed by new product demands, sales teams burned out by unrelenting targets, customer service departments drowning in volume—these are not simply operational missteps, they are structural failures born from an assumption that the strongest part of the business can take infinite strain.

Scaling at the edges takes a different view. It begins with the recognition that *the core is precious and fragile*, even when it appears robust. The systems, cultural norms, and decision-making rhythms at the centre are the foundation on which everything else stands. Overload them, and you risk undermining the very stability that allowed the company to grow in the first place. By contrast, targeted expansion into adjacent markets, supplementary services, or peripheral capabilities allows the company to test growth hypotheses in controlled environments, absorbing lessons and refining models before applying them more broadly.

Consider how Amazon approached its now-iconic Prime membership. At launch, it was not a reinvention of its retail core but an edge experiment—an offering layered onto existing operations to deepen customer loyalty and increase purchase frequency. The programme's infrastructure demands were significant but not destabilising; they built on existing logistics and product availability. Over time, Prime evolved into a platform that reshaped the company's economics and strategic direction, but its introduction did not require tearing apart the existing retail operation. This principle holds across sectors: expansion that starts in a contained, adjacent space can evolve into a transformative force without creating chaos.

The discipline in edge scaling lies in recognising what is genuinely adjacent versus what is a disguised leap. For example, a software-as-a-service company adding a complementary analytics tool is working at the edges; the engineering, sales, and support demands overlap with existing competencies. That same company deciding to launch an unrelated hardware device is not edge scaling—it is venturing into a new domain that demands entirely different expertise, supply chains, and risk management. The difference matters because scaling at the edges works by *leveraging existing strengths while stretching capacity in manageable increments.*

Edge growth also offers a powerful testing ground for cultural resilience. New initiatives can attract different customer segments, require alternative sales narratives, and call for new workflows. By launching them on the periphery, leaders can observe how the organisation adapts to change without destabilising the main engine. These insights are invaluable for identifying cultural weak points, operational bottlenecks, and leadership gaps before those issues are amplified in the core business. This kind of iterative learning is almost impossible when every available resource is consumed by a massive, centre-driven expansion.

Another advantage of scaling at the edges is its ability to insulate the brand from reputational risk. Core operations carry the weight of customer expectations; a significant failure there can inflict lasting damage. Peripheral ventures, while still linked to the brand, offer more room to experiment and occasionally fail without catastrophic consequences. The hospitality industry offers clear examples: hotel chains that test new service models or technology-enabled experiences in select properties before rolling them out globally can contain the fallout of missteps while still positioning themselves as innovators.

It is also worth noting that edge scaling can be a strategic hedge against market volatility. When core markets contract, peripheral revenue streams—especially those that are counter-cyclical or serve different customer profiles—can help maintain stability. During the

COVID-19 pandemic, many restaurants survived by rapidly scaling edge operations such as takeaway, delivery-only kitchens, or meal kit services. These adaptations were not replacements for the core dining experience, but they provided critical cash flow and, in some cases, opened new permanent revenue channels.

The execution of scaling at the edges requires a different mindset from traditional expansion planning. First, it demands a rigorous understanding of core capacity—what systems, teams, and processes can comfortably handle today, and where the breaking points lie. Leaders must resist the temptation to "borrow" capacity from the core to feed edge experiments if doing so compromises existing performance. Second, it requires clarity of purpose: each edge initiative should serve a strategic objective, whether that is entering a new market segment, testing a technology, or diversifying revenue. Vague ambitions to "see what happens" invite wasted resources and diluted focus.

Funding strategies for edge scaling also differ. Because these initiatives are often exploratory, they should be financed in ways that reflect their experimental nature—ringfenced budgets, limited exposure to core cash flow, and milestone-based investment release. This protects the main business from uncontrolled cost creep while keeping the pressure on edge teams to validate their impact. In many cases, treating these initiatives as internal start-ups—with their own leadership, metrics, and accountability—creates the right balance of autonomy and alignment.

However, edge scaling is not without its hazards. Poorly managed, it can create cultural rifts, especially if edge teams are seen as privileged or disconnected from the daily realities of the core business. To avoid this, leaders must invest in communication that frames edge initiatives as collective opportunities rather than elite projects. Integrating cross-functional contributions, celebrating shared wins, and making the learning loop visible to the wider organisation all help prevent the emergence of an "us versus them" mentality.

Ultimately, scaling at the edges is about resisting the false dichotomy between aggressive central growth and defensive stability. It acknowledges that an organisation can remain anchored while still exploring new territory, provided that exploration is disciplined, strategically aligned, and proportionate to available capacity. This approach requires patience, because its wins often accumulate over time rather than delivering instant surges. Yet the payoff is growth that strengthens rather than strains, and a business that emerges from expansion not just bigger, but more adaptable and resilient.

The founders and executives who master this approach recognise that sustainable growth is as much about protecting the core as it is about reaching new frontiers. By treating the edges as the proving ground for the future, they create a portfolio of opportunities that can be scaled into the centre when the organisation is ready—ensuring that, when the moment comes, the core is not destabilised but fortified.

Chapter 6
The Founder as Chief Communicator

For many founders, leadership begins in the tactile realm: building a product, assembling a team, and shaping the contours of a fledgling company. Yet as an enterprise grows—and particularly once external capital enters the equation—the nature of that leadership must evolve. The founder becomes, in effect, a communicator-in-chief. This is far from a ceremonial title. Words, framing, and narrative take on weight equal to strategy and execution. Boards, investors, employees, customers, regulators—all interpret signals differently, yet all are influenced by the way those signals are conveyed. A founder adept at this can buy time, secure alignment, and marshal support in situations where raw operational performance might fall short. Neglect it, and the story of the company is written for you, often in ways that serve others' interests more than your own.

The boardroom provides the most visible theatre for this dynamic. A meeting is never a simple recitation of facts; it is a carefully staged environment where data and narrative compete for dominance. Founders who grasp this understand that the sequence of information, the context it is placed in, and the confidence with which it is delivered all shape both immediate decisions and longer-term perceptions of competence. This is not manipulation—it is synthesis. Numbers do not speak for themselves; they require interpretation, and in the boardroom, the founder assumes the role of interpreter-in-chief. A temporary revenue shortfall, framed as a brief deviation within an otherwise healthy trend, evokes a far different investor response than the same shortfall presented in isolation as a stark deficit. Both are factual; only one preserves momentum and confidence.

Investor updates suffer a similar misconception, often reduced to perfunctory reporting. In truth, these updates are strategic levers. Each monthly or quarterly communication is a rare, structured opportunity to influence how investors perceive the company. They offer a platform to highlight progress that raw numbers alone cannot capture, to steer attention toward leading indicators, and to shape investor focus in alignment with the company's strategic horizon.

Treat updates as a chore, and engagement will be equally shallow; treat them as an ongoing campaign of narrative shaping, and investors become allies who can champion the company in forums the founder will never attend. Subtle choices—the milestones highlighted, the sequence of information, even tone—often determine whether an investor perceives control and competence or uncertainty and risk.

The most advanced application of this skill is storytelling as a mechanism for alignment. Founders operate at the centre of a web of stakeholders whose objectives do not always align. Crafting a unifying narrative turns disparate concerns into shared goals. When revenue is under pressure, a founder might feel compelled to reassure investors with cost-control plans, energise employees with promises of innovation, and calm customers with service guarantees—all simultaneously. Without a coherent narrative, these messages fragment, leaving each audience with its own interpretation and, worse, its own anxieties. The founder's task is to identify the common thread—the challenge that, once addressed, benefits all parties—and frame it in a manner that catalyses coordinated action. Narrative, in this sense, becomes strategic glue, requiring an ability to see the company through multiple lenses simultaneously.

Crisis magnifies this responsibility. Communication becomes a primary instrument for buying time to stabilise operations, secure capital, or recalibrate strategy. Skill lies not in platitudes but in measured disclosures. Share too little, and credibility erodes; share too much, and panic or opposition may spread. Effective crisis communication rests on two principles: clarity and containment. Clarity ensures stakeholders understand both the nature of the issue and the concrete steps being taken; containment ensures the problem is not amplified beyond its true scope. An earnings shortfall presented with transparent context and a credible recovery plan preserves trust; the same shortfall, framed vaguely or defensively, can trigger cascading doubt that is difficult to reverse.

Mastery of these arenas—boardroom influence, investor updates, narrative alignment, and crisis messaging—requires more than charisma or eloquence. It demands preparation, data fluency, and the discipline to remain consistent across multiple communications without slipping into predictability. Founders who inhabit this role fully gain more than reputation; they acquire strategic leverage. They create buffers during setbacks, accelerate buy-in for new initiatives, and reinforce the perception that they control both the business and its story. In ventures where investor confidence can matter as much as cash flow, this leverage can decide the line between survival and collapse.

This chapter approaches communication with the same rigour applied to operational planning or financial modelling. It does not treat it as an abstract art, but as an integrated discipline requiring systems, repeatable processes, and constant refinement. By its conclusion, the goal is not to produce a more polished speaker or writer in isolation, but to equip founders to wield communication deliberately, as a strategic instrument of leadership. In a business world where perception often shapes reality, mastery of this craft is not optional—it is foundational.

Boardroom as Theatre: Crafting compelling, data-backed narratives for investor meetings

Every board meeting is a performance. The setting may be corporate, the participants may be wearing suits rather than costumes, and the dialogue may be shaped by numbers rather than scripts, but the dynamics are theatrical in every meaningful sense. There is staging—the order in which slides appear, the sequencing of agenda items, the moment a particular chart is revealed. There is audience management—reading the expressions of the room, sensing when to accelerate a point, when to pause, when to let silence work. And there is narrative—the framing of data so that the figures do not merely exist in isolation, but connect into a coherent story that leads towards the decisions the founder wants made. In high-stakes environments, *how* information is presented often shapes the outcome as much as the information itself.

Founders who approach board meetings as pure reporting exercises tend to miss this truth. They assume their role is to deliver facts accurately and in full, believing transparency will inevitably lead to rational decisions. In practice, information without narrative leaves interpretation—and therefore power—in the hands of others. A founder who simply lays out the numbers invites board members to build their own mental models of the business, often informed by their biases, past experiences, or unrelated portfolio companies. The result is a meeting that can drift off-course, dominated by questions and debates that might not align with the company's priorities. *The most effective founders enter the room with a clear understanding of the story they want the board to leave with—and they engineer every data point, chart, and anecdote to reinforce that story.*

This does not mean bending facts. It means *choosing the context* in which they are understood. Consider the case of a startup whose customer acquisition cost has risen by 20% in the past quarter. Presented without context, this triggers alarm. Framed alongside data showing that lifetime customer value has simultaneously doubled due to a new retention initiative, it becomes a positive development—a sign that the company is winning more valuable customers, even at a higher cost. The numbers in both versions are identical, but the narrative framing changes the meaning entirely. Effective boardroom storytelling anticipates these points of potential misinterpretation and addresses them *before* they can become distractions.

Preparation here is both analytical and theatrical. Analytically, the founder must identify the metrics that matter most to the board's decision-making, understand the relationships between those metrics, and anticipate questions from different vantage points—financial, operational, market-level. Theatrically, they must decide the pacing: which wins to surface early to create momentum, which challenges to acknowledge once credibility has been established, and where to place the critical ask or strategic pivot so that it lands with maximum clarity and conviction. In this sense, the board deck is not just a container of information; it is a designed experience, guiding the audience through a sequence of intellectual and emotional beats.

The "data-backed" aspect of this work is where many founders overcompensate. They assume that more data equals more credibility. In reality, *selectivity* builds trust more than data dumps. A board presented with thirty dense slides of metrics is unlikely to remember—or care about—most of them. A board shown three or four high-leverage metrics, each supported by a crisp narrative that explains its trajectory and implications, is far more likely to engage constructively. The discipline lies in deciding which data matters most to the story being told, then supporting it with just enough additional detail to withstand scrutiny without derailing the narrative.

The theatre metaphor extends beyond slides and sequencing into the founder's presence in the room. Delivery matters: posture, tone, eye contact, and even the strategic use of pauses. An overly defensive tone when presenting weaker metrics can amplify investor concern. Over-enthusiasm about a minor win can feel like overcompensation. The best communicators modulate their delivery to signal both confidence and self-awareness—celebrating wins without bravado, acknowledging setbacks without surrender. They also recognise that the boardroom is as much about listening as speaking. Knowing when to hold the floor and when to step back, letting an idea circulate and gain unspoken agreement, is a subtle but critical skill.

Real-world examples illustrate the stakes. In one well-known case, a late-stage technology company faced an impending shortfall on aggressive revenue targets. The founder could have led with the deficit, braced for criticism, and allowed the meeting to devolve into post-mortem analysis. Instead, they opened with an update on an unexpectedly strong product adoption curve in a secondary market, showing early signs of significant lifetime value. Only after building the case for the market's potential did they reveal the shortfall—framed as a conscious trade-off to invest more heavily in the emerging opportunity. By the end of the meeting, the board had not only endorsed the shift in focus but approved additional investment. The data had not changed, but the sequence and framing had transformed it from a problem into a strategy.

There is also a cautionary dimension. Poorly managed boardroom theatre can backfire. A founder who over-stages the meeting, suppressing uncomfortable facts until they are inevitably uncovered, will lose credibility far faster than one who lays them out early with a clear plan for resolution. Similarly, an over-polished presentation that feels scripted to the point of inauthenticity can create distance rather than trust. The key is *calibrated transparency*: enough openness to earn confidence, enough narrative control to maintain direction. This balance is not static; it shifts with the maturity of the company, the composition of the board, and the macro environment in which the business operates.

Ultimately, treating the boardroom as theatre is not about performance for its own sake. It is about recognising that investor meetings are high-leverage moments in the life of a company, where the perception of control, competence, and trajectory can influence strategic decisions as much as actual performance. Founders who enter the room without a script—or worse, with a script divorced from the company's reality—cede that influence to others. Founders who master the craft can align their boards more effectively, secure backing for bold moves, and shape the narrative that follows the company outside the boardroom walls. In ventures where capital, time, and patience are finite resources, that mastery can prove decisive.

Investor Updates as Influence Tools: Turning quarterly reports into strategic levers for shaping perception and buy-in

Quarterly investor updates are among the most underutilised strategic tools in a founder's arsenal. Too often, they are treated as compliance exercises—obligations to be discharged by sending a spreadsheet-heavy PDF and a few paragraphs of commentary. In this view, updates are retrospective: a backward glance at the quarter that was, offered in the spirit of transparency. Yet in the hands of a skilled communicator, these updates can serve a far more powerful function. They can become forward-tilting narratives, subtly shaping investor perception, reinforcing strategic priorities, and building the kind of buy-in that ensures smoother decision-making and greater latitude in moments of uncertainty. *Every investor update is an opportunity not only to inform, but to influence.*

The distinction between information and influence lies in framing. Information alone tells investors what happened; influence helps them interpret what happened in a way that aligns with the company's intended direction. This is not a matter of manipulation—it is a matter of narrative leadership. Investors, even the most analytical, make judgements within a context shaped by how events are presented. The same set of numbers can feel like either a disappointment or a calculated bet depending on whether the update positions them as deviation from plan or as an intentional shift in resource allocation toward a bigger, longer-term prize. Founders who understand this dynamic craft their updates with the discipline of political speechwriters: precise in detail, careful in sequencing, and attentive to the underlying emotional as well as rational currents in the audience.

The tone of the update sets the relationship temperature. An overly cautious, numbers-only tone—devoid of colour or insight—can create distance, leaving investors to form their own narratives, often drawing on imperfect analogies from other portfolio companies. Conversely, updates that over-rotate into hype and optimism can breed scepticism if they fail to acknowledge real challenges. *The most effective updates balance candour with conviction*—they surface problems early enough to maintain trust, but always within a framing that reinforces the founder's grasp of the situation and commitment to resolution. Investors are far more forgiving of setbacks when they are given a coherent explanation and a credible recovery plan than when they are presented with selective good news and evasive omissions.

One critical but underappreciated function of these updates is expectation management. Between formal board meetings, investors may have little to no structured contact with the company's inner workings. Their mental model of the business is sustained largely by the quarterly rhythm of updates. When updates are inconsistent in style, content, or focus, that mental model becomes unstable—and unstable expectations tend to manifest as surprise objections or unanticipated resistance when major decisions arise. By contrast, *consistently structured, thoughtfully prioritised updates create a shared frame of reference over time,* making it easier to secure agreement on strategic pivots, additional funding, or operational changes when they become necessary.

Practical structuring matters here. A strong update begins by reaffirming the company's strategic priorities, then reports progress and setbacks through that lens. This sequencing ensures that numbers are interpreted in context rather than in isolation. For instance, if one of the stated priorities is deepening market penetration in a high-value segment, the update might open with qualitative and quantitative evidence of traction in that segment—even if headline revenue growth is slower overall. By leading with the strategic intent, the founder signals control and intentionality, shaping how investors weigh each metric.

Timing also plays a role in influence. While quarterly is the norm, some founders opt for monthly or bi-monthly touchpoints in periods of rapid change or heightened investor concern. This can be especially valuable in transitional phases such as post-funding ramp-ups, major product launches, or market shocks. Frequent, high-quality updates during these periods can pre-empt anxiety, head off rumours, and reduce the risk of reactive decision-making from the investor side. The key is not simply increasing the volume of communication but maintaining the same standard of clarity, framing, and strategic alignment in each touchpoint.

Real-world examples highlight the power of this approach. A health-tech startup, facing a temporary drop in user acquisition due to a regulatory shift, used its quarterly update to reframe the issue not as a growth stall but as a validation of its long-term compliance-first positioning. The update led with an investor-ready narrative: a reminder that the company's strategy was to outlast less prepared competitors in a market where regulatory credibility would become a decisive differentiator. By including forward-looking indicators—pipeline contracts contingent on the new compliance framework—the update transformed what could have been read as a warning sign into evidence of a durable moat. Investors, rather than pressing for immediate fixes, doubled down on their support for the company's measured approach.

There is, however, a danger in treating every update as an exercise in spin. Investors are generally sophisticated enough to detect over-polished narratives that leave no room for uncertainty. The absence of any bad news can be more damaging than the admission of a controlled setback. Founders who use updates solely as a stage for positive reinforcement risk eroding trust, particularly when inevitable surprises emerge later. The art lies in *owning the challenges as much as the wins,* presenting them within a framework that demonstrates not only awareness but proactive response. This transforms perceived weakness into proof of resilience and operational competence.

Another underleveraged dimension of investor updates is their role in social proof within the investor network. Updates are rarely read in isolation; they circulate informally among co-investors, potential investors, and strategic partners. A well-crafted update can subtly position the company in the broader market narrative—signalling momentum, market relevance, and leadership even before a funding round is announced. Conversely, a weak or erratic update cadence can undermine the company's standing, making it harder to rally support when needed. Recognising that *every update is potentially part of a wider conversation* encourages founders to invest in clarity, cohesion, and strategic messaging even when the audience seems limited to the current cap table.

Ultimately, the influence power of quarterly investor updates stems from their dual nature as both operational reports and relationship touchpoints. They are a forum for conveying performance, but also a stage for reinforcing alignment, building confidence, and pre-positioning the company's future moves. Founders who approach them as strategic levers—rather than obligatory recaps—can subtly shape the mental and emotional landscape in which critical decisions are made. And in ventures where timing, consensus, and perception often determine whether the next bold step is funded or stalled, that shaping can be as decisive as the numbers themselves.

Storytelling for Stakeholder Alignment: How to frame challenges so investors, executives, and teams work toward the same solution

The most dangerous moment in a company's growth is not when a challenge emerges, but when the people responsible for addressing it each hold a different mental model of what the challenge is and what success looks like. Misalignment doesn't always announce itself as outright conflict; it often manifests as quiet divergence—investors focusing on capital efficiency while executives chase top-line growth, or teams prioritising short-term delivery at the expense of long-term capability. The founder's job is to prevent these divergences from calcifying, and one of the most effective tools for doing so is strategic storytelling. *A well-constructed narrative can collapse competing interpretations into a single shared frame, creating a coordinated push toward the same outcome.*

The mechanics of this alignment go beyond inspiration. Effective stakeholder storytelling operates at the intersection of fact and framing. Facts are non-negotiable; they give credibility and prevent the narrative from being dismissed as spin. But the framing determines how those facts are prioritised, sequenced, and imbued with meaning. The same set of financial figures, for example, could be presented to investors as evidence of market dominance or as a warning of margin compression—depending entirely on which elements the story places in the foreground and how it links them to the company's overarching objectives. When a founder is deliberate about this framing, they can guide investors, executives, and frontline teams to focus on the same levers rather than working at cross-purposes.

The challenge is that different stakeholders inhabit different temporal and cognitive horizons. Investors often evaluate through the lens of return timelines and risk exposure. Executives operate within operational and strategic cycles, balancing quarterly targets against multi-year positioning. Teams live in the immediacy of deliverables, dependencies, and day-to-day trade-offs. *An effective founder's narrative bridges these horizons,* showing each group how their efforts fit into the broader arc without diluting the clarity of their individual mandates. For example, during a period of intentional slowdown in customer acquisition to prioritise product stability, the investor-facing story might emphasise protecting the long-term unit economics, while the internal story focuses on creating the conditions for more sustainable scaling. The message is tailored, but the underlying truth—the shared rationale—remains constant.

To build such narratives, founders need to identify the core tension in the challenge and articulate it in a way that makes resolution a common priority. This requires stripping away the noise of departmental perspectives and isolating the underlying cause that, if addressed, would move all metrics in the right direction. Consider a logistics startup facing delivery delays. Operations may see the bottleneck as staffing shortages, investors as capital inefficiency, and product teams as a technology gap. A unifying story might frame the challenge as "scaling reliability without inflating costs," presenting data that connects staffing, capital allocation, and system improvements as interdependent solutions. The framing shifts the focus from siloed fixes to a coordinated set of actions, each stakeholder seeing their role as part of the same solution pathway.

This is where narrative discipline matters. The temptation in times of stress is to flood stakeholders with exhaustive detail, hoping that transparency will produce alignment. In practice, *overloading audiences with unfiltered information can fragment interpretation rather than unify it.* A disciplined narrative filters for relevance, structuring information so that each piece reinforces the central thesis. In the delivery-delay example, that might mean leading with a single unifying metric—on-time delivery percentage—and showing how each corrective action impacts it, rather than dumping raw data on staffing ratios, vehicle availability, and API response times without synthesis.

A particularly powerful alignment technique is to reframe challenges as part of a strategic inevitability rather than as isolated crises. Founders who can position obstacles as predictable phases of the company's evolution often gain more patience and constructive engagement from stakeholders. For example, a SaaS company experiencing churn after introducing a higher pricing tier could frame this not as a failure of product-market fit but as the expected turbulence of moving upmarket, with churn concentrated among price-sensitive customers who were never the long-term target segment. This framing not only reassures investors that the strategy is intact but also motivates teams to refine features for the more valuable customer base rather than scramble to win back the departing cohort.

Real-world cases illustrate how poor storytelling can deepen misalignment. A consumer tech company, after missing growth targets, issued separate communications to investors and teams—one emphasising external market headwinds, the other focusing on internal execution gaps. While each message was partly true, the inconsistency bred suspicion. Investors questioned whether leadership was avoiding accountability, while teams felt demoralised by what seemed like a mismatch between external and internal narratives. A single, coherent story—acknowledging both market shifts and execution gaps, and showing the coordinated actions to address them—could have prevented the erosion of trust.

Founders must also be alert to the emotional dimension of alignment. Rational alignment on strategy is fragile if stakeholders feel excluded, undervalued, or blindsided. The most resonant narratives often acknowledge these emotional undercurrents without being sentimental. This could mean explicitly recognising the strain on teams during a strategic pivot, or validating investor concerns about burn rate before explaining the rationale for continued investment in a long-cycle initiative. *By showing that you understand both the head and the heart of the audience, you increase the likelihood that they will commit to the course you set.*

There is a philosophical aspect here too: storytelling for alignment is not about manufacturing consensus; it is about making the best path forward visible enough that consensus becomes the natural response. That requires humility—being willing to expose uncertainties and trade-offs—and confidence in equal measure. It also requires the discipline to ensure that, over time, the story evolves consistently, so that each update feels like the next chapter of an unfolding plan rather than a disconnected episode.

When done well, this form of storytelling becomes a stabilising force in the company's culture and governance. Investors begin to trust that they will be brought into the loop with clarity and foresight, reducing the tendency to micromanage. Executives start to anticipate the founder's framing and adjust their own departmental communications accordingly. Teams see a clear through-line from leadership's vision to their daily work, which strengthens motivation and resilience. In effect, the founder's story becomes the operating system that integrates the perspectives of diverse stakeholders into a single, coordinated execution.

The absence of such storytelling has the opposite effect: investors push for short-term wins that undermine long-term positioning, executives chase conflicting KPIs, and teams oscillate between priorities, burning resources without cumulative progress. In the volatile environment of a scaling company, this misalignment can be fatal—not because of the challenge itself, but because of the incoherence in tackling it. The founder who masters the art of framing challenges so that everyone works toward the same solution doesn't just solve individual problems more effectively—they build the alignment infrastructure that makes future challenges easier to face together.

Crisis Messaging: What to say—and not say—when performance dips

The moment a company's performance falters, the quality of its messaging can determine whether it emerges with credibility intact or spirals into deeper instability. A dip in revenue, customer retention, or operational efficiency is rarely fatal in itself; what erodes trust is the mishandling of the narrative. Investors, employees, customers, and the public do not expect perfection, but they do expect clarity, coherence, and a signal that leadership is in control of both the facts and the plan forward. *The real test in a downturn is not whether you can explain what happened, but whether you can do so without creating more uncertainty than you resolve.*

The first principle in crisis communication is to resist the urge to over-sanitise the story. A performance dip inevitably triggers speculation; when leadership offers only vague reassurances or superficial explanations, it invites stakeholders to fill the gaps themselves, often with worst-case assumptions. Yet the opposite extreme—over-disclosure without discipline—can overwhelm and fragment the audience's understanding. *The most effective crisis messages balance transparency with curation: enough detail to build credibility, but anchored to a clear, digestible narrative that keeps focus on the path forward rather than drowning in post-mortem minutiae.*

Consider the contrast between two public company earnings calls after a poor quarter. In one, the CEO offers a high-level acknowledgment of missed targets, attributes them vaguely to "market headwinds," and pivots quickly to talking points about the company's long-term vision. Investors leave unconvinced, reading the evasiveness as a sign that the situation may be worse than disclosed. In the other, the CEO identifies specific causal factors—

such as a delayed product launch in a key region and a sharp increase in supply costs—before outlining the concrete steps underway to mitigate them, including renegotiating supplier contracts and reallocating marketing spend. The latter not only clarifies what went wrong, but also demonstrates that leadership is actively managing the resolution.

What is *not* said can be as consequential as what is. Ill-chosen omissions—particularly those later revealed through leaks, filings, or independent analysis—can destroy credibility far faster than a poor result ever could. Founders and executives must therefore test their messaging against the likelihood of undisclosed information surfacing later. If the gap between public statements and eventual revelations is too wide, the crisis shifts from operational underperformance to a perceived integrity failure. That reputational damage is far harder to recover from than a temporary dip in the numbers.

The framing of the message also matters deeply. Leaders often default to defensive positioning, overemphasising external factors—regulation changes, economic cycles, competitor actions—as if to absolve themselves of responsibility. While contextualising performance is valid, *stakeholders draw confidence from leaders who balance external context with ownership of the company's response.* Even if market conditions played a significant role, the narrative should make clear how the organisation is adapting, not simply how it was disadvantaged. The subtext of a strong crisis message is: "We understand the problem, we own the problem, and we have the means to address it."

Timing is another critical variable. A delayed acknowledgment of performance issues can fuel suspicion that leadership either failed to detect the problem early or hoped to conceal it. Both interpretations erode trust. Rapid communication, even if initial details are provisional, signals vigilance and commitment to transparency. However, speed without preparation is equally risky; a hasty, incoherent statement can lock the company into a poorly framed narrative that is difficult to unwind later. The optimal approach is to prepare a provisional, fact-checked message as soon as key indicators point to a material deviation from expectations, paired with a commitment to provide fuller updates as more data emerges.

Internally, the stakes are just as high. Employees are often the first to sense when performance is slipping, and silence from leadership breeds rumour, anxiety, and attrition. Internal crisis messaging must therefore do more than echo the external talking points; it should address the specific concerns of the workforce, explain how the company's response affects their roles, and outline what is expected of them in the recovery effort. *A workforce that feels informed and engaged is far more likely to channel its energy into solutions rather than speculation.*

The tone of delivery is equally influential. Stakeholders can detect the difference between confident candour and scripted deflection. Over-rehearsed language, corporate jargon, and evasive phrasing undermine authenticity. Conversely, a conversational but precise style—acknowledging uncertainty where it exists while being definitive where facts are established—builds credibility. In this context, the messenger matters; having the founder or CEO deliver the message in person, whether via a live call, recorded video, or in-room meeting, signals accountability and personal investment in the outcome. Delegating the communication entirely to investor relations teams, legal counsel, or mid-level managers dilutes that signal.

One underutilised tool in crisis messaging is the *pre-emptive narrative.* If leadership has been consistently communicating both successes and setbacks along the way, a performance dip can be framed as a known risk that has now materialised rather than an unforeseen disaster. This softens the blow, as stakeholders have been mentally prepared for volatility and can place the current moment in a longer arc of execution. For instance, if a founder has previously discussed the potential revenue lag following a strategic pivot, then when that lag arrives, the update is not a shock—it is a checkpoint.

Equally important is the disciplined avoidance of over-promising in the recovery plan. The instinct to reassure can tempt leaders into setting aggressive timelines or targets that may not be realistic. Missing these secondary promises can cause more damage than the original miss, reinforcing perceptions of unreliable leadership.

Instead, the message should set achievable milestones, each of which can be publicly met, building momentum and restoring credibility incrementally.

Crisis messaging is not solely about external perception; it is about operational leverage. A clear, credible narrative can secure investor patience, maintain employee morale, and buy the time needed to implement corrective measures. A poor one accelerates capital withdrawal, talent loss, and competitive exploitation of perceived weakness. Founders and executives who master the art of saying enough—but not too much—while framing both problem and solution with integrity are far better positioned to turn temporary underperformance into a proving ground for leadership.

Ultimately, when performance dips, the right words do not simply describe reality—they actively shape the conditions under which recovery takes place. A founder who can articulate the setback with candour, frame it with context, and pair it with a disciplined plan earns the space to fix the underlying issue. One who mishandles the message risks turning a temporary challenge into a permanent fracture in stakeholder trust.

Chapter 7
Strategic Constraint as a Competitive Advantage

For most founders, leadership begins with creation—a product, a team, a company. Yet as the enterprise expands, particularly once external capital arrives, the founder's role morphs from builder-in-chief to communicator-in-chief. This is far from a ceremonial distinction. Words, framing, and narrative acquire significance on par with strategy and execution. Boards, investors, employees, customers, regulators—each interprets signals differently, yet all are influenced by how those signals are conveyed. A founder who masters this dimension can buy crucial time, secure alignment, and garner support where raw performance alone might falter. Ignore it, and the company's story is written for you, often in ways that serve others' interests more than your own.

The boardroom exemplifies this dynamic. Meetings are rarely simple exchanges of facts; they are carefully staged arenas where data and narrative vie for dominance. Founders who understand this recognise that the sequence of information, the context into which it is placed, and the confidence with which it is delivered shape not only immediate decisions but also ongoing perceptions of competence and control. This is not manipulation—it is synthesis. Numbers do not speak for themselves; they require interpretation, and the founder assumes the role of chief interpreter. A revenue shortfall framed as a brief dip within a fundamentally sound trend elicits a very different response from investors than the same shortfall presented as a bare deficit. Both are factual; only one preserves momentum and confidence.

Investor updates are similarly misunderstood, often relegated to mere reporting chores. In reality, these communications are strategic levers. Each quarterly or monthly update is one of the few structured opportunities to shape how investors perceive the company. They allow founders to highlight progress invisible in raw numbers, to draw attention toward leading rather than lagging indicators, and to align investor focus with the strategic horizon the company has chosen. Treat updates as a perfunctory task, and engagement will be shallow; treat them as ongoing exercises in narrative shaping, and investors become allies who can champion the company in arenas the founder will never reach. Often, the difference between an investor who believes "they've got it under control" and one who worries "this is a problem" lies in subtle cues: the milestones emphasised, the sequencing of updates, even the tone of written summaries.

The most advanced form of founder communication, however, is storytelling as a tool for alignment. Founders operate at the centre of a web of stakeholders whose goals do not always coincide. Crafting a unifying narrative transforms divergent concerns into shared objectives. When revenue is under pressure, for instance, a founder might feel compelled to reassure investors with cost-control measures, motivate employees with promises of innovation, and calm customers with service guarantees—all at once. Without a coherent narrative, these messages fracture, leaving each audience with its own interpretation and, worse, its own anxieties. The founder's task is to identify the common thread—the challenge that, once addressed, benefits all parties—and to frame it in a manner that drives coordinated action rather than competing agendas. Narrative, in this sense, becomes strategic glue, demanding an ability to see the company through multiple lenses simultaneously.

During crises, this responsibility intensifies. Communication becomes the principal tool for buying time to stabilise operations, secure capital, or recalibrate strategy. Skill lies not in platitudes but in calibrated disclosures. Reveal too little, and credibility erodes; reveal too much, and panic or opposition may spread. The best crisis communicators adhere to two principles: clarity and containment. Clarity ensures stakeholders understand both the nature of the issue and the concrete steps being taken. Containment ensures the perceived scope of the problem does not expand beyond reality. An earnings shortfall presented with transparent context and a credible recovery plan preserves trust; the same shortfall, framed vaguely or defensively, can trigger cascading doubt that is difficult to reverse.

Mastering these arenas—boardroom performance, investor updates, narrative alignment, and crisis messaging—requires more than charisma or eloquence. It demands preparation, data fluency, and the discipline to maintain consistency across multiple communications without slipping into predictability. Founders who inhabit this role fully gain more than reputation; they acquire strategic leverage. They create buffers during setbacks, accelerate buy-in for new initiatives, and reinforce the perception that they command both the business and its story. In ventures where investor confidence matters as much as cash flow, this leverage can spell the difference between survival and collapse.

This chapter examines these dimensions with the same rigour applied to operational planning or financial modelling. Communication is not treated as an art form separate from business execution but as an integrated discipline—requiring systems, repeatable processes, and continuous refinement. By the conclusion, the aim is not to make the founder a better speaker or writer in isolation, but to equip them to wield communication deliberately, as a strategic instrument of leadership. In a world where perception often shapes reality, mastery of this skill is not optional; it is foundational.

The Discipline of Saying No: Protecting focus when investor enthusiasm pushes for expansion into too many markets or products

The most seductive form of pressure a founder will ever face comes not from competitors or customers, but from well-intentioned backers eager to fund rapid expansion. It is rarely framed as recklessness. On the contrary, it is often packaged in the language of opportunity—"the market is hot," "we can dominate if we move now," "let's not let this window close." This enthusiasm, particularly in moments of favourable momentum, can feel almost impossible to resist. Yet saying yes to every promising lead is often the first step towards undermining the very conditions that made the business investable. The discipline to say no—to decline or defer expansion even when capital is abundant and external confidence is high—is not an act of caution so much as an assertion of control over the company's strategic narrative. *The refusal is not about rejecting growth; it is about rejecting growth that dilutes the organisation's ability to execute at the highest level in the arenas where it matters most.*

The underlying danger of overexpansion is not simply that it stretches resources thin; it is that it fractures the company's attention. In the early years, most successful founders operate with almost monastic focus: every conversation, every hire, every engineering sprint is directed at a clearly defined target. That focus compounds—operational systems are fine-tuned, product-market fit is sharpened, and cultural norms are reinforced through consistent repetition of priorities. Expansion into new markets or products introduces a second, then a third, then a fourth set of priorities. These begin to compete with one another for leadership bandwidth, capital allocation, and organisational energy. The result is not merely slower progress on each front, but the erosion of the cohesion that made initial successes possible. It is a dilution of excellence into adequacy.

There is a psychological trap here, compounded by investor psychology. Many backers are optimised for portfolio theory—they are comfortable spreading bets, knowing that some will fail as long as others return outsized gains. A founder, however, cannot afford to manage their own company as though it were just one of many lottery tickets. Each new initiative represents a personal and organisational bet that, if lost, affects not only capital but credibility, morale, and the company's reputation in the market. This asymmetry means that what feels like prudent diversification to an investor may amount to dangerous overreach for a founder. *It is precisely in moments of investor optimism that the founder must become the chief risk filter, protecting the business from opportunities it is not yet structurally prepared to pursue.*

The discipline of saying no often requires reframing the definition of opportunity itself. Founders tend to think of opportunities as things to be seized before they vanish. In reality, the most strategic opportunities tend to persist, or even improve, when approached at the right moment. Entering a new geography before local operational competence exists may secure early market share, but it also risks building a fragile foundation—alienating customers through poor execution and allowing better-prepared competitors to displace the company later. The disciplined leader asks: not "Can we enter now?" but "Can we enter now without compromising our executional standard or eroding our advantage in the core business?"

This shift turns the decision from an emotional race against time into a sober assessment of readiness.

Case histories illustrate both sides of this equation. Consider the contrast between two well-funded consumer brands launched within the same decade. One, flushed with early venture capital, launched five product lines and entered multiple international markets within three years. Each product line achieved initial sales, but operational inconsistency, mounting returns, and a diffusion of marketing resources left none with category dominance. Within five years, the company was forced into restructuring, its brand equity damaged. The other, equally well-capitalised, refused multiple overtures from investors to expand beyond its core product and home market until its operational systems, brand recognition, and supply chain resilience met internally defined thresholds. When it did expand, it did so sequentially—one adjacent category, one new market at a time—allowing each to reach profitability before launching the next. The second company's growth curve was slower in the early years, but its brand became synonymous with quality in its niche, enabling sustainable international expansion later with far less competitive resistance.

This is not an argument against ambition; it is an argument for sequencing. Ambition without sequencing produces fragility; ambition with sequencing produces compounding strength. The ability to say no is therefore a corollary to the ability to identify the one or two strategic battles worth winning at any given time. This is why some of the most disciplined leaders maintain explicit "not doing" lists alongside their strategic roadmaps. Such lists act as internal safeguards against the seduction of the possible, forcing leaders to articulate and defend the reasons for deferring certain initiatives until predefined criteria are met. This approach transforms "no" from a reactive refusal into a deliberate, premeditated component of the growth strategy.

Cultural reinforcement is critical here. An organisation's willingness to say no at the leadership level must be mirrored throughout its ranks. If teams believe that leadership's strategic focus is merely rhetorical—that any enthusiastic pitch can win funding—they will begin to dilute their own priorities, hedging their attention across multiple speculative projects. Over time, this creates a culture of distraction in which deep work is displaced by shallow experimentation. By contrast, when leadership consistently models and communicates the reasons behind strategic refusals, teams internalise the value of depth over breadth. They learn that success is not measured by the number of initiatives launched, but by the impact of those that succeed.

Finally, it is worth noting that the discipline of saying no often requires more political skill than operational skill. Turning down an investor's pet idea, or deferring a high-profile market entry that the board is excited about, can strain relationships. The founder must therefore cultivate the ability to reject without alienating—to explain refusals in terms of protecting long-term value, sequencing for maximal impact, and safeguarding the investor's own capital from premature risk exposure. This is not pandering; it is reframing constraint as a form of protection and stewardship. The most credible leaders can show, with data and a compelling narrative, that their restraint is not timidity but precision.

The irony is that a founder's refusal to overextend in the short term often increases investor confidence in the long term. A company that grows deliberately, building strength and optionality with each step, becomes a far safer and more attractive platform for future investment. What begins as an uncomfortable "no" can, when explained and executed well, strengthen both the company's strategic position and its relationship with its backers. *Saying no, then, is not simply an act of resistance; it is an investment in the conditions that make future yeses more powerful and more sustainable.*

Resource Allocation as Strategy: Making deliberate trade-offs to protect your most promising growth engines

The hardest decisions a founder makes are rarely about what to pursue—they are about what to deprioritise, slow, or cut entirely. Capital is never as abundant as ambition, and even when a business is well-funded, the capacity of leadership teams, operational infrastructure, and organisational focus is finite. Every resource allocation decision is therefore a strategic act, not a mechanical one. The difference between companies that scale into enduring market leaders and those that burn brightly before fading is often the difference between spreading resources thinly across all attractive opportunities and concentrating them deliberately in the areas most likely to compound long-term advantage. *Saying yes is easy; saying yes to one thing and no to three others is the work of strategy.*

The problem for most founders is that allocation decisions are frequently made under conditions of asymmetrical pressure. Investors may be pushing for aggressive expansion, while internal teams lobby for the resources to explore new features, markets, or products. Competitors, meanwhile, create a sense of urgency by moving quickly in adjacent spaces. In such an environment, allocation decisions are at risk of becoming reactive—determined more by who makes the loudest case than by a disciplined analysis of where each marginal unit of capital, talent, and time will yield the greatest strategic return. Effective founders resist this noise. They recognise that *resources are multipliers only when concentrated; dispersed, they become dampeners, blurring momentum instead of accelerating it.*

Consider the example of a high-growth enterprise SaaS company that, flush from a successful Series C round, faced simultaneous opportunities: launching into Europe, building a machine learning add-on requested by a major client, and expanding its mid-market offering. Each had compelling business cases, each had vocal champions. Rather than split engineering, marketing, and sales resources across all three, the CEO commissioned a rigorous analysis of projected cash flows, customer acquisition costs, and the degree to which each initiative reinforced or diluted the company's core positioning. The result: full resource commitment to the European launch, with the machine learning project moved to a skunkworks team operating under strict constraints, and the mid-market push deferred entirely for 18 months. The decision frustrated some stakeholders, but within two years the European expansion was generating revenue on par with the North American base, providing the financial and operational strength to tackle the other two opportunities with greater confidence and capacity.

The key insight is that resource allocation is not only about financial capital. Human capital—especially leadership attention—is often the scarcer currency. A founder's time is not infinitely divisible, and spreading it across multiple initiatives inevitably dilutes their influence and decision-making sharpness in each. Similarly, the cognitive and emotional energy of the broader leadership team is a finite resource. Allocating senior talent to one growth engine means intentionally under-allocating to others, which in turn requires the discipline to accept slower progress—or even stagnation—in those areas. This is uncomfortable, particularly in high-performance cultures that prize constant motion, but it is also essential. *Focus is less about choosing the best opportunity; it is about accepting the cost of ignoring good ones.*

What makes resource allocation particularly strategic is that it is inherently tied to sequencing. Rarely is a "no" forever—it is often a "not yet." The discipline lies in resisting the temptation to run multiple plays in parallel when the organisation is better served by stacking them sequentially. This sequencing compounds not just learning but capability. Each successful execution increases the company's operational sophistication, brand credibility, and cash reserves, making the next initiative more likely to succeed. Conversely, launching multiple initiatives before the organisation has the absorptive capacity to handle them risks creating a string of half-completed, underperforming projects that undermine investor confidence and internal morale alike.

Philosophically, deliberate resource allocation is an act of identity as much as economics. Where a company chooses to invest is a signal—both internally and externally—about what it values and where it believes its competitive advantage lies. Allocating disproportionately to a particular product line, market, or customer segment tells employees where to innovate, tells customers where the company's expertise is deepest, and tells investors where returns will be maximised. This signalling effect is powerful, but it also cuts both ways: incoherent or inconsistent allocation erodes trust and creates strategic ambiguity, leading stakeholders to question whether leadership truly has a clear plan.

One of the most underappreciated aspects of resource allocation is the role of opportunity cost in shaping competitive dynamics. If two companies in the same sector each have £50 million to deploy, but one commits £30 million to dominating a single vertical while the other spreads £10 million into each of five, the concentrated player will almost always establish a deeper moat faster. That moat—built on superior customer experience, market share, and operational efficiency—becomes the foundation for subsequent expansions. The diffused player, by contrast, risks becoming the second-best option in multiple markets, vulnerable to displacement by more focused rivals. This is why deliberate trade-offs are not a constraint on growth; they are a precondition for durable growth.

A counterpoint worth considering is that some businesses have successfully pursued multiple growth engines simultaneously—often cited examples include Amazon's parallel development of retail, cloud computing, and logistics capabilities. Yet such cases tend to involve extraordinary leadership capacity, massive capital reserves, and a culture engineered for relentless execution across diverse domains. Even then, these companies built each engine to a level of maturity before heavily resourcing the next. AWS, for instance, grew quietly for years before becoming the focus of large-scale capital and talent allocation. The lesson for most founders is not to emulate the scale of such diversification, but to recognise that even the giants sequence their bets more carefully than is often assumed.

Protecting the most promising growth engines, then, is as much about defence as offence. It means shielding these engines from being starved of attention when new ideas emerge, ensuring that their momentum is not eroded by shifting priorities. This often requires formal mechanisms: dedicated budgets that are insulated from reallocation raids, locked-in timelines for delivering on key milestones before resources are diverted elsewhere, and clear, non-negotiable performance metrics that justify continued investment. It also requires the founder to act as the chief advocate for these engines in the face of competing demands—repeatedly articulating why they remain central to the company's strategic advantage and long-term valuation.

Ultimately, resource allocation as strategy is about embracing the reality that leadership is a constant exercise in selective neglect. You cannot give everything equal attention, and the attempt to do so is one of the most common causes of avoidable failure. By deliberately concentrating resources where they will have the highest multiplier effect—and by having the courage to defend those decisions against the pressures of novelty, politics, and opportunism—a founder not only protects their most promising growth engines but ensures that the company's story, internally and externally, remains coherent, compelling, and investable. *Growth is not simply a function of what you choose to pursue; it is defined by what you are willing to leave behind for now.*

Selective Risk-Taking: How to take calculated bets without jeopardising core stability

The most dangerous misconception about entrepreneurial success is that it belongs to those who take the biggest risks. In reality, sustained success belongs to those who take *the right risks, at the right time, with the right safeguards.* Recklessness masquerading as courage is an indulgence that early-stage founders can ill afford, and even less so as the business matures. The problem is not risk itself—every act of growth is inherently risky—it is the failure to differentiate between risks that strategically strengthen the business and those that silently undermine its foundations. *The real skill is not in avoiding uncertainty, but in structuring it so that it cannot destroy you.*

Selective risk-taking begins with a clear understanding of the organisation's core stability—its non-negotiable foundations that must remain intact regardless of market turbulence or strategic experimentation. For a consumer brand, this might be supply chain reliability and brand trust; for a software company, it could be uptime performance and user data security; for a medical device manufacturer, regulatory compliance and clinical credibility. These pillars form the perimeter around which risks can be taken. You can experiment aggressively in areas that do not compromise them, but breaching them even once can trigger reputational and operational damage that is impossible to reverse. *Strategic risk is about placing bets at the edges, not gambling with the centre.*

One of the most effective mental models for selective risk-taking is borrowed from portfolio theory: treat your core business as the conservative, income-generating portion of a portfolio, and your growth experiments as the higher-volatility investments that can yield outsized returns. The size of the "experimental" allocation depends on the maturity, cash reserves, and market position of the business. In earlier stages, the tolerance may be higher because there is less to defend; in later stages, the allocation shrinks proportionally as the cost of destabilising the core increases. This is why many scaled businesses use an 80/20 or even 90/10 split between resources allocated to core operations and those reserved for high-risk initiatives. The discipline lies in not allowing short-term enthusiasm or investor pressure to reverse these ratios without hard evidence that the upside justifies it.

History offers cautionary examples. In the early 2000s, BlackBerry dominated the smartphone market, but instead of selectively experimenting with touchscreens and consumer-focused design, it doubled down almost exclusively on enterprise security—a core strength, but without placing small, calculated bets on emerging trends. When the market shifted, it had no tested alternatives to scale. Contrast this with Netflix's calculated pivot into streaming: the company maintained its DVD rental operations as a revenue-stable core while funnelling a manageable portion of capital and talent into building the streaming infrastructure. By the time DVD rentals began to decline, the streaming business was already proven, scalable, and supported by internal expertise.

A selective approach to risk also requires acknowledging that not all risks are equal in time horizon, reversibility, or visibility. Some risks—such as launching a marketing campaign in a new demographic—are relatively low-cost and reversible if early signs are poor. Others—such as building a new manufacturing facility or re-architecting core software infrastructure—are deep-commitment moves that, once initiated, cannot easily be undone. Selective risk-takers tend to stage higher-cost bets through reversible early phases, using pilot projects, limited market tests, or time-boxed exploratory work to gather evidence before committing fully. This approach preserves optionality: the freedom to scale a winning bet or cut a losing one without collateral damage.

The tension between core stability and risk appetite often surfaces most sharply in board discussions, especially after funding rounds. Investors, particularly those with shorter fund cycles, may push for bold plays that accelerate market capture. The founder's role is to channel that ambition into a risk structure that does not compromise long-term survivability. This means insisting on pre-defined kill criteria for experimental initiatives, securing ring-fenced budgets that prevent cost overruns from bleeding into core operations, and ensuring that leadership accountability for risky projects is explicit. Without these guardrails, the organisation risks what might be called "risk creep"—where a contained experiment gradually expands in scope and resource drain without clear evidence of viability.

Selective risk-taking is not simply about scale of investment; it is also about the degree of strategic alignment. A bet that reinforces and extends existing advantages is inherently safer than one that requires building entirely new capabilities from scratch. For instance, when Apple entered the wearables market with the Apple Watch, it was not a leap into the unknown—it leveraged existing competencies in hardware design, user experience, and brand loyalty. The upside was significant, but the downside was cushioned by the fact that even if the Watch had failed commercially, it would not have threatened Apple's core iPhone business. By contrast, a hypothetical pivot into, say, automotive manufacturing would carry a vastly different risk profile because it would demand a set of core capabilities the company did not already possess at the time.

Philosophically, selective risk-taking is rooted in probabilistic thinking. Founders must resist the seductive clarity of binary thinking—the assumption that a bet will either "work" or "fail"—and instead weigh the spectrum of possible outcomes, the likelihood of each, and the impact on the organisation's trajectory. This mindset allows for bolder action in areas where the downside is minimal even if the probability of success is low, and greater caution where the downside is existential even if the probability of failure is small. In other words, it is not enough to ask, "What if it works?"—you must also ask, "What if it doesn't, and what will be left standing?"

Critically, selective risk-taking thrives in cultures that are able to separate the evaluation of the decision from the outcome. A well-structured, data-informed, strategically aligned bet can still fail because of external shocks or unpredictable shifts. Punishing teams for these failures discourages intelligent experimentation; instead, leaders should reward the rigour of the process, ensuring that future bets benefit from the accumulated learning. Over time, this builds a portfolio of institutional knowledge that increases the quality of risk assessment and execution, reducing the variance of outcomes even in high-uncertainty domains.

What separates the mature founder from the impulsive one is not the absence of ambition, but the ability to channel that ambition into risk structures that maximise learning while safeguarding survival. Selective risk-taking allows companies to explore the edges of their opportunity space without drifting into existential danger. It is the difference between lighting small, controlled fires to clear the underbrush and torching the entire forest in the hope that something better grows in its place. The best founders understand that stability and risk are not opposing forces—they are interdependent. Stability provides the platform from which risk can be taken with confidence, and risk, when managed well, provides the discoveries that keep stability from ossifying into complacency. *Growth without risk is fantasy; risk without stability is suicide.*

Constraint-Driven Innovation: How limitations often drive sharper innovation than abundance

It is tempting to believe that the surest path to innovation lies in removing every obstacle—providing teams with unlimited budget, unrestricted time, and unrestricted access to talent and resources. Yet history tells a different story: many of the most transformative innovations have emerged not from abundance but from scarcity, not from freedom without boundaries but from the pressure of constraint. The paradox is that limitation often sharpens ingenuity rather than dulling it, because it forces clarity of thought, prioritisation of effort, and the imaginative repurposing of what is already at hand. *Constraints strip away the indulgence of the obvious and compel the search for the truly original.*

This principle is visible in fields as diverse as aerospace engineering, product design, and software development. Consider the Apollo 13 mission: when an oxygen tank exploded mid-flight, the astronauts and NASA ground crew were left with crippled life-support systems, dwindling power, and a spacecraft never designed for such contingencies. There was no possibility of "throwing more resources at the problem"; every kilogram and watt was finite. The solution—

constructing a CO_2 scrubber from spare parts and improvised materials already on board—was a direct consequence of working under severe, non-negotiable constraints. Far from paralysing the team, the limitations gave their problem-solving a laser-like focus, accelerating decision-making and enabling survival.

In a business context, the same dynamic plays out when companies face capital constraints, regulatory restrictions, or compressed timelines. While abundance allows for parallel exploration of multiple options, it also enables waste: pet projects that are never killed off, features added without strategic justification, and solutions over-engineered beyond their real utility. Constraints force hard trade-offs, making it necessary to determine which customer needs truly matter, which design elements genuinely drive adoption, and which channels actually produce results. In this way, scarcity acts as an unrelenting filter, stripping away nice-to-haves until only the high-leverage essentials remain.

The most effective founders learn to wield constraints not merely as unfortunate realities but as deliberate strategic tools. Limiting resources can be used to accelerate time to market by preventing over-polishing; restricting scope can foster product simplicity and focus; enforcing headcount caps on certain teams can maintain agility by ensuring that decision-making remains concentrated rather than diffused across layers of management. *Self-imposed constraints can be as valuable as externally imposed ones, provided they are designed with intent rather than as cost-cutting measures alone.*

Consider the case of the early days of Southwest Airlines. Operating in a heavily regulated industry with a shoestring budget, the airline could not afford the inefficiencies of traditional carriers. Constraints—both financial and operational—led to a radical rethinking of the business model: a single aircraft type for operational simplicity, no assigned seating to reduce turnaround times, and a point-to-point route structure that avoided the complexity of hub-and-spoke systems. These limitations became not just coping mechanisms but competitive advantages, enabling cost leadership and operational reliability that endured long after the initial scarcity eased.

This is not to say that constraints are universally beneficial. Some limitations, particularly those that choke off access to critical talent or essential infrastructure, can create false economies that harm long-term viability. The difference lies in whether the constraint drives creative reconfiguration or forces damaging compromise. The challenge for leadership is to distinguish between constraints that foster innovation and those that cripple it. This requires honest appraisal: if a constraint pushes the organisation to find a better way of achieving the same goal, it is likely valuable; if it consistently results in reduced quality or undermines trust, it is destructive and must be removed.

One reason constraint-driven innovation works is that it changes the problem space from one of unlimited possibilities to one that can be mentally and operationally contained. Abundance creates a combinatorial explosion of options, increasing decision fatigue and slowing execution. Constraints reduce this noise, making it easier to evaluate trade-offs and commit to a course of action. Psychologists have long observed that creativity flourishes within boundaries: a blank canvas can be paralysing, but a specific prompt—whether a set colour palette or a restricted set of materials—can ignite focus and experimentation. In organisational terms, the equivalent is a clear set of non-negotiables around budget, time, or operational parameters that provide a stable frame within which teams can experiment freely.

Technology companies have repeatedly demonstrated this principle under resource limitations. Instagram's original team of fewer than 15 people built a platform capable of handling millions of daily uploads not because they had the largest budgets, but because their infrastructure limitations forced them to optimise relentlessly for performance and scalability from the outset. By contrast, well-funded start-ups often fall into the trap of overbuilding early systems under the illusion that they can "fix it later," leading to bloated architectures and technical debt that take years to unwind. The constraint forces a discipline of simplicity that abundance often erodes.

Constraints also have a cultural dimension. In well-led organisations, they create a shared urgency and sense of purpose. People rally more readily when the stakes are high and the parameters are clear, because every decision feels consequential. This shared urgency fosters cross-functional collaboration—departments that might otherwise work in silos are compelled to pool expertise to overcome a common limitation. In such environments, innovation is not the responsibility of a designated "R&D team" but a collective, distributed behaviour. When managed poorly, however, the same constraints can generate burnout and resentment, particularly if employees perceive them as arbitrary or unfair. The framing of the limitation—whether it is presented as an opportunity to innovate or merely as a burden to endure—has a profound impact on whether it drives ingenuity or demoralisation.

From a strategic perspective, constraint-driven innovation can also serve as a defence against the complacency that often follows market success. Established companies with ample resources are at risk of falling into incrementalism—making marginal improvements to existing products and processes while disruptive innovation happens elsewhere. Introducing selective constraints, such as fixed innovation budgets, limited release cycles, or tightly defined problem statements, can help these organisations recapture the urgency and focus of their start-up phase without artificially impoverishing themselves. Google's famous "20 per cent time" is, paradoxically, a constraint—it limits the time available for exploratory work, forcing employees to focus their innovation energy into a narrow window rather than scattering it across the workweek.

In the long term, the healthiest approach is to treat constraints as variables that can be tuned to match the needs of the moment. Early-stage companies may operate under near-constant constraint due to external necessity; scaling companies can apply self-imposed constraints selectively to maintain agility; mature enterprises can use targeted constraints to drive innovation in specific areas without destabilising the whole. The most skilful leaders are those who can calibrate these levels dynamically—tightening or loosening constraints as the strategic environment shifts—while keeping the organisation's inventive capacity consistently high.

Ultimately, constraint-driven innovation is not about celebrating hardship for its own sake. It is about recognising that abundance can be as dangerous as scarcity if it dulls the edge of focus and urgency. Limitations—when intelligently designed or constructively embraced—do not just force us to do more with less; they force us to do *better with less.* They compel choices that might otherwise be deferred indefinitely, sharpen the questions we ask, and elevate the standards by which we measure our solutions. Far from being a brake on progress, the right constraints can be the engine that drives it.

Chapter 8
Managing the Board Without Being Managed

For most founders, leadership initially manifests through creation—a product, a team, a company. Yet as the organisation expands and external capital enters the equation, the role subtly but significantly shifts: from builder-in-chief to communicator-in-chief. This is far from ceremonial. The currency of influence changes. Words, narrative, and framing now carry weight equal to strategy and execution. Investors, boards, employees, customers, regulators—each interprets signals differently, yet all respond to how those signals are delivered. A founder who masters this dimension can buy time, secure alignment, and galvanise support where performance alone might fall short. Neglect it, and the story of the company is written for you, often to your detriment.

The boardroom offers the clearest lens into this dynamic. Meetings are rarely mere exchanges of facts; they are carefully orchestrated arenas where data and narrative vie for attention. The most effective founders understand that the order of presentation, the context in which information is framed, and the confidence of delivery shape both immediate decisions and the ongoing perception of competence. This is not manipulation—it is synthesis. Numbers alone do not speak; they demand interpretation, and the founder assumes the role of chief interpreter. A revenue shortfall framed as a temporary deviation within a fundamentally sound trendline elicits a markedly different investor response than the same shortfall presented as a bare deficit. Both are accurate; only one preserves momentum and confidence.

Investor updates, too, are often misunderstood as mere obligations. In truth, they are strategic levers. Each quarterly or monthly report represents one of the few structured opportunities to influence how investors perceive the company. These updates allow founders to highlight progress invisible in raw numbers, to emphasise leading rather than lagging indicators, and to align investor focus with the company's chosen strategic horizon. Treat updates as a chore, and engagement will be minimal; treat them as a carefully managed campaign of narrative framing, and investors can become advocates in rooms the founder will never enter. Often, the difference between an investor thinking "they've got it under control" and one worrying "this is a problem" lies in subtle cues: the milestones highlighted, the sequencing of updates, even the tone of written summaries.

The most sophisticated form of founder communication, however, lies in storytelling as a mechanism for alignment. Founders sit at the nexus of stakeholders whose interests do not always align naturally. Crafting a unifying narrative converts divergent concerns into shared objectives. When revenue pressures mount, the instinct may be to reassure investors with cost controls, energise employees with innovation promises, and calm customers with service guarantees—all simultaneously. Without a coherent narrative, these messages fracture, leaving each audience with its own interpretation, and often its own anxiety. The founder's task is to identify the common thread—the challenge which, once addressed, benefits all—and to frame it in a way that generates coordinated action rather than competing agendas. Narrative, in this sense, becomes strategic glue, demanding an ability to see the company from multiple perspectives at once.

In times of crisis, this responsibility intensifies. Communication becomes the primary instrument for buying time to stabilise operations, secure capital, or adjust strategy. Skill lies not in platitudes but in calibrated disclosure. Say too little, and credibility erodes; say too much, and panic—or opportunism—may spread. The most effective crisis communicators adhere to two principles: clarity and containment. Clarity ensures stakeholders understand both the problem and the concrete steps being taken. Containment ensures the message does not exaggerate the scope of the issue. An earnings miss explained with context and a credible recovery plan preserves trust; the same shortfall framed vaguely or defensively can trigger cascading doubt that is difficult to reverse.

Mastery of these arenas—boardroom performance, investor updates, narrative alignment, and crisis messaging—requires more than charisma. It demands preparation, data fluency, and discipline to maintain consistency across multiple communications without falling into predictability. Founders who inhabit this role fully gain more than reputation; they acquire strategic leverage. Words can create a buffer during setbacks, accelerate buy-in for initiatives, and reinforce the perception that the founder commands both the business and its story. In ventures where investor confidence is as critical as cash flow, that leverage can decide survival or collapse.

This chapter examines these dimensions with the same rigour applied to operational planning or financial modelling. Communication is treated not as a separate art form but as an integrated discipline—requiring systems, repeatable processes, and constant refinement. The goal is not simply to make the founder a better speaker or writer in the abstract, but to enable them to wield communication deliberately, as a strategic instrument of leadership. In a world where perception often shapes reality, mastery of this skill is not optional—it is foundational.

The Board's True Purpose: Dispelling Myths About the Board's Role and Influence

Many founders misinterpret the board as an extension of their executive team, a kind of elite advisory group whose primary function is to validate strategy and unlock networks. Others view it with suspicion, as a looming authority poised to undermine their autonomy. Both perspectives are flawed, and both can prove costly. A board is neither a rubber stamp nor a shadow management committee; its authority is both narrower and deeper than most leaders initially realise. Understanding the true purpose of the board is essential not only to making it work for the company, but also to protecting the founder's position and vision.

The legal foundation of the board's role is governance. Directors are charged with safeguarding the company's long-term interests, ensuring that the organisation operates within legal and ethical boundaries, and that it remains financially sound. This fiduciary duty—to act in the best interest of the shareholders as a whole—is not a slogan but a binding obligation. It is here that many misunderstandings arise. Founders often believe their board exists to champion their vision at all costs, but the board's loyalty is ultimately to the company, not to the founder. When performance falters or strategic disputes emerge, the board's role shifts from cheerleader to guardian of the enterprise, and those who mistake personal alignment for institutional duty can be caught off guard.

Another persistent myth is that the board exists primarily to guide operational decisions. While directors can provide valuable insight on specific matters, their involvement should remain strategic, not tactical. A well-functioning board challenges assumptions, stress-tests strategy, and provides an external perspective informed by a diversity of experience. What it must avoid is slipping into management mode, directing hiring choices, micromanaging product development, or setting sales targets. This blurring of boundaries is common in early-stage companies, where boards are small and often populated by investors who feel a direct stake in operational outcomes. The danger is that founders start managing the board's operational preferences rather than running the company according to market realities.

In reality, the most effective boards operate as disciplined stewards of governance and strategic risk management. They ensure that capital is deployed wisely, that major commitments are made with due consideration, and that the company is not blind to threats—whether competitive, regulatory, or internal. Their role is to interrogate strategy without dictating it, to scrutinise performance without becoming the performance. For founders, this distinction is critical: allowing the board to perform its true function can lead to sharper decision-making, better risk calibration, and more resilient long-term positioning. Treating it as an executive body in disguise undermines both governance and operational autonomy.

Real-world cases illustrate the consequences of misunderstanding the board's role. Consider the high-profile implosion of several well-funded start-ups where boards were content to serve as passive endorsers during rapid expansion, only to intervene abruptly when revenue slowed or regulatory scrutiny mounted. In these situations, the board's late-stage assertiveness felt like betrayal to founders, but from a governance perspective, it was a delayed correction of years of insufficient oversight. The reverse can be just as damaging: boards that involve themselves too deeply in day-to-day decisions can stifle agility, slow product cycles, and sap the founder's ability to lead decisively. Both extremes arise when the board's purpose has not been clearly defined, agreed, and reinforced over time.

Understanding purpose is only half the challenge; the other half is shaping expectations. This is where founders have more influence than they realise. By framing discussions around strategic priorities, circulating pre-reads that highlight key decision points, and explicitly stating where they seek input versus where they will make the final call, leaders can help their boards stay anchored in their true remit. This framing does not diminish the board's authority; it channels it productively. A board grounded in well-structured dialogue is far less likely to drift into operational interference or to retreat into passivity.

The healthiest founder–board relationships are built on a mutual recognition of roles. The founder brings deep, real-time knowledge of the business, operational control, and the capacity to execute. The board brings external perspective, governance discipline, and the authority to hold leadership accountable. When each side respects the other's domain, the result is a strategic partnership that enhances, rather than constrains, performance. This partnership is not symmetrical—ultimate decision-making power rests with the board—but it can be balanced. Founders who understand that balance are better equipped to protect their vision while benefiting from the oversight that investors, regulators, and markets expect.

Dispelling myths about the board's role is not simply an academic exercise. It changes the way a founder prepares for meetings, selects directors, and communicates strategy. It shapes how conflicts are navigated and how trust is built. A board that understands its purpose acts as a stabilising force in moments of volatility and a credible check on overreach in moments of euphoria. For the founder, clarity on this point is the difference between being supported and being sidelined. And in the high-stakes environment of scaling a company, that distinction can decide not just the fate of the leadership, but the trajectory of the enterprise itself.

Pre-Meeting Engineering: How to Prepare and Pre-Align Members Before Formal Meetings

The outcome of a board meeting is rarely decided in the boardroom itself. By the time the agenda is called to order, positions have been formed, alliances have been tested, and the gravitational pull of opinion is already shaping the discussion. Founders who treat the meeting as the primary battleground for decisions are often blindsided by dynamics they could have influenced days or weeks earlier. The real strategic work lies in what happens before the meeting begins: in the quiet, deliberate process of pre-meeting engineering.

Pre-meeting engineering is not manipulation, nor is it about manufacturing consensus for its own sake. It is about ensuring that the most important conversations happen in an informed, thoughtful, and less performative environment—where nuance can be explored without the distortion of group theatre. Formal meetings tend to amplify the loudest voices and compress complex issues into binary votes. Outside those meetings, however, stakeholders are more open to discussing subtleties, admitting uncertainties, and reconsidering their positions without the pressure of a live audience.

The first principle is clarity of purpose. Too many leaders send pre-reads filled with operational minutiae, expecting directors to sift out the real decision points on their own. This is not pre-alignment; it is abdication. A founder who knows exactly what they need from the board—whether it is approval for a capital raise, endorsement of a strategic pivot, or a reframing of performance expectations—can distil the context and stakes into a concise framing that guides every pre-meeting conversation. *Pre-meeting clarity does not mean overloading members with data; it means equipping them with the right data, in the right order, for the decision at hand.*

Timing is equally critical. Contacting a director the day before the meeting with a sensitive proposal is rarely effective; positions harden quickly when decisions feel rushed. Instead, a staggered approach—beginning with those most likely to be neutral or supportive, then moving to potential dissenters—allows the founder to test arguments, refine responses, and understand where compromise may be necessary. These early discussions are diagnostic: they reveal whether opposition is rooted in principle, in incomplete information, or in interpersonal dynamics. The response strategy differs in each case.

One overlooked element of pre-meeting engineering is managing the sequence of influence. In most boards, certain members set the tone for others—not through formal authority, but through credibility, reputation, or personal relationships. Securing the informal leaders first can prevent the meeting from being swayed by a single well-timed objection. The inverse is also true: if a dissenting voice with influence is left unaddressed, they can rally others against the proposal before the meeting even begins. A founder who understands this hierarchy of influence treats pre-meeting conversations as an intentional order of engagement, not a random outreach list.

Case studies from high-growth companies illustrate the stakes. In one instance, a CEO seeking approval for international expansion spent weeks in one-on-one calls with directors, walking through market entry plans and addressing concerns about regulatory risk. By the time the proposal reached the formal agenda, every major objection had already been aired and addressed; the meeting was a confirmation, not a debate. Contrast this with another company where a founder unveiled a major acquisition proposal cold in a board meeting. Two directors voiced immediate doubts, and the rest, unwilling to appear uncritical, joined in. The acquisition collapsed—not because the deal lacked merit, but because the founder failed to prepare the terrain.

Pre-meeting engineering also extends to the design of the meeting itself. Strategic founders use the agenda as a structural tool, placing contentious items after areas of agreement to build momentum, or framing proposals within broader strategic priorities to avoid narrow, tactical debates. They anticipate not just the content of the discussion, but its rhythm: which issues need space for reflection, where quick resolutions are possible, and when to close before fatigue sets in. By discussing this sequencing with key members beforehand, the founder turns the meeting into an exercise in guided decision-making rather than an open-field skirmish.

The ethical boundary in pre-meeting work lies in representation. Mischaracterising other directors' positions, omitting material information, or applying undue pressure erodes trust and damages long-term credibility. The goal is not to win every vote, but to ensure that votes are cast with the best possible understanding of the facts, the risks, and the trade-offs. When pre-meeting alignment is done well, even those who ultimately dissent respect the process, because they were engaged as participants rather than presented as obstacles.

At its core, pre-meeting engineering is an act of respect—for the time of the board, for the quality of the decisions, and for the strategic integrity of the company. It acknowledges that the most consequential decisions demand more than a two-hour exchange in a formal setting; they require a thoughtful build-up, an informed cast of decision-makers, and a leader who sees the meeting not as the stage for persuasion, but as the final scene of a well-prepared play. Founders who master this discipline do more than improve their odds of securing support—they elevate the entire quality of governance, creating a boardroom where the formal vote is merely the logical conclusion of a process that began long before the meeting was called to order.

Board Composition Strategy: Choosing Directors Who Balance Expertise, Network, and Temperament

The quality of a company's board is rarely the result of chance; it is almost always the product of deliberate, sometimes painstaking, design. The mistake many founders make is treating board appointments as functional checkboxes—fill the finance seat, find an industry veteran, secure a respected investor nominee—and assume that the sum of these credentials will naturally yield effective governance. In practice, the composition of the board shapes not only the calibre of strategic advice but also the tone, pace, and resilience of decision-making. A board built purely for technical brilliance without attention to interpersonal chemistry can become paralysed by conflict. Conversely, a board chosen for harmony at the expense of challenge risks becoming a rubber stamp. The art lies in balancing expertise, network, and temperament in a way that strengthens the company across both predictable and volatile circumstances.

Expertise is the most visible and quantifiable dimension of board composition, but even here, nuance is essential. Too many boards lean on narrow definitions of what constitutes relevant expertise—defaulting to sector veterans who have spent decades in the same competitive frame. While such directors can offer valuable pattern recognition, they may also carry entrenched assumptions that make them less open to unconventional strategies. For high-growth or disruptive companies, the most valuable expertise often comes from adjacent sectors, where directors can bring transferable insights without being constrained by the orthodoxy of the industry in question. The selection process must interrogate not just what a potential director knows, but how they think, how they learn, and whether they can apply their knowledge fluidly to new contexts.

Network, in this context, is not simply a contact list; it is the director's ability to open doors that the company could not realistically access otherwise. This might mean introductions to strategic partners, customers, regulators, or future investors. Yet the value of a network is not proportional to its size—it is determined by its relevance, depth, and the director's willingness to deploy it. Some directors guard their relationships, offering them sparingly, while others actively broker connections that advance the company's objectives. The founder's task is to distinguish between the *perceived* network of a high-profile name and the *activated* network of someone deeply invested in the company's success. In the latter case, the network becomes a living asset rather than a line on a biography.

Temperament is often treated as an afterthought—something nice to have if the candidate already ticks the other boxes—but in the reality of board dynamics, it can be the decisive factor in whether the group functions effectively under pressure. A board member's temperament influences how they process disagreement, how they respond to incomplete or ambiguous information, and how they balance assertiveness with openness. In moments of crisis, a director who can bring measured calm, maintain intellectual curiosity, and avoid defensive posturing is worth more than an encyclopaedia of industry knowledge. This is not about avoiding conflict; the best boards embrace robust debate. It is about ensuring that conflict sharpens thinking rather than degenerating into factionalism.

One of the challenges in balancing these three dimensions is that they do not always coexist naturally in a single individual. A director with unparalleled technical expertise may have a limited network or an abrasive style that requires active management. A well-connected diplomat may lack the depth to interrogate complex strategic proposals. This is why composition must be approached as a portfolio problem, not an exercise in finding mythical all-rounders. The goal is to assemble a board where the collective balance of expertise, network, and temperament covers the company's needs—and where the members' strengths and weaknesses are complementary rather than redundant.

An effective founder will also anticipate how the board's needs will evolve. The composition that serves a company at Series A will not necessarily serve it at pre-IPO stage. For example, a start-up expanding into regulated markets may require the addition of a director with deep regulatory relationships, even if that means rotating out someone whose contributions were more relevant in an earlier phase. This is a politically delicate process, but avoiding it out of loyalty or inertia can stunt the company's progression. The most disciplined boards embrace renewal as a sign of maturity, not disloyalty.

The strategic design of a board also extends to diversity—not as a performative exercise, but as a pragmatic advantage. Diversity of professional background, geography, gender, and cognitive approach broadens the lens through which opportunities and risks are evaluated. Homogeneous boards are more prone to groupthink, overconfidence, and blind spots. However, diversity without a unifying strategic culture can be equally dangerous, leading to fragmented priorities. The founder's role is to ensure that the board's diversity fuels constructive challenge within a shared understanding of the company's mission and constraints.

Practical application of these principles requires a level of rigour that most founders underestimate. Reference checks must go beyond verifying a candidate's CV; they should probe how the candidate behaves in high-stakes situations, how they handle dissent, and whether they have a track record of following through on offers of assistance. Informal conversations with former colleagues or co-directors can reveal patterns invisible in formal interviews. Equally, founders should make their own expectations explicit from the outset—detailing not just the governance responsibilities, but the level of engagement, availability, and responsiveness expected. This upfront alignment reduces the likelihood of misinterpretation and underperformance later.

Case history offers ample cautionary tales. One scaling tech firm, eager to impress prospective investors, recruited a high-profile former CEO to its board. His credentials were impeccable, but his approach was combative and dismissive of the younger management team. His presence dominated meetings, silencing other directors and eroding the collaborative culture. By contrast, another company in the same sector appointed a less famous but deeply engaged director with a background in adjacent markets; she leveraged her network to secure pivotal partnerships and acted as a stabilising influence during a turbulent leadership transition. In both cases, the impact of the appointment far exceeded what could be predicted from a résumé—proof that the human element can be as decisive as the technical one.

Ultimately, board composition is one of the few levers a founder can pull that will continue to shape the company long after day-to-day control has been diluted. The right mix of expertise, network, and temperament not only enhances decision quality but also builds a governance environment capable of adapting to shifting landscapes. Founders who approach this as a strategic design problem, rather than a series of opportunistic appointments, position their boards—and by extension, their companies—not just to survive scrutiny, but to harness it as a source of enduring strength.

Board Politics in Practice: Recognising and Managing Alliances, Rivalries, and Hidden Agendas

The formal language of board governance—fiduciary duties, strategic oversight, shareholder alignment—presents an image of rational, impartial stewardship. Yet anyone who has spent time inside a functioning boardroom knows that beneath this layer of procedure lies a dense web of interpersonal politics. These politics do not exist in spite of the board's professionalism; they are the inevitable by-product of bringing together influential individuals with divergent incentives, reputations to protect, and personal interpretations of what is "best" for the company. *Ignoring these dynamics is not a mark of integrity—it is a strategic blind spot that can undermine even the most compelling business plan.*

Alliances within boards form for a variety of reasons: shared professional backgrounds, overlapping investment interests, philosophical alignment on strategy, or simply the familiarity bred from years of working together in other contexts. Such alliances can be a stabilising force when they unite members behind bold but necessary decisions, particularly in times of uncertainty. They can also distort governance when loyalty to a relationship outweighs commitment to the company's best interests. A founder who understands the informal power map of the board can predict how key votes will break, who will influence whom, and where potential fractures might emerge. Without that awareness, they risk being blindsided by decisions shaped not by the quality of argument but by pre-existing loyalties.

Rivalries, on the other hand, often emerge less from open ideological clashes than from subtler competitions for influence. Two directors may agree on most issues yet still vie for primacy in shaping the company's direction or in positioning themselves as the board's most valuable voice. In some cases, rivalries trace back to historic professional tensions—failed partnerships, contested deals, or reputational conflicts carried over from previous roles. These tensions can manifest in the undermining of colleagues' proposals, pointed questioning that edges into personal territory, or behind-the-scenes lobbying to sway other members. A skilled founder learns to distinguish between rivalries that, while uncomfortable, generate constructive tension, and those that threaten to paralyse decision-making through entrenched opposition.

Hidden agendas are more elusive, partly because they are rarely articulated in full. Not every director's priorities align perfectly with the stated mission of the company. An investor-appointed director may subtly push for an exit timeline that serves their fund's liquidity needs rather than the optimal long-term growth trajectory. A corporate representative might be less interested in the company's standalone success and more focused on securing strategic leverage for their parent organisation. Even ostensibly independent directors may carry quiet ambitions—to enhance their profile in the market, to use the board seat as a stepping stone to other opportunities, or to advance causes aligned with their personal brand. The danger lies not in the existence of these agendas—they are, in truth, unavoidable—but in failing to detect them early enough to anticipate their influence on strategy.

Recognising these dynamics demands more than careful listening during formal meetings. Board politics live in the interstices: in pre-meeting calls, informal dinners, private emails, and chance encounters at industry events. Founders who rely solely on what is said at the table are only seeing the visible portion of the decision-making process. The most effective leaders maintain active lines of communication with directors between meetings—not to manipulate outcomes, but to understand shifting positions, emerging concerns, and the mood of the group. These conversations can reveal when a director's stance is softening, hardening, or being influenced by another member's persuasion.

Managing alliances, rivalries, and hidden agendas requires a blend of diplomacy and decisiveness. A founder cannot—and should not—attempt to neutralise every political current; doing so risks turning the role into a reactive firefight. Instead, they must decide which dynamics to engage with directly, which to allow to play out, and which to subtly counterbalance through board composition or agenda-setting. This might mean pre-emptively engaging a sceptical director before a contentious vote to address concerns privately, thereby removing fuel from a potential public clash. It might mean structuring meeting agendas so that sensitive items are preceded by discussions where consensus is easier to reach, creating a cooperative atmosphere before entering high-stakes debates.

One of the most underused tools in this arena is the cultivation of independent alliances—relationships that cut across existing factions. When a founder earns the trust of individual directors from different camps, they can act as a bridge between them, framing issues in ways that reduce polarisation. Over time, this reduces the risk that decisions are shaped purely along factional lines. The founder's credibility is central here: trust erodes quickly if directors perceive them as playing one side against the other for personal advantage.

Case studies illustrate how acute the stakes can be. In one mid-stage SaaS company, the CEO underestimated the influence of a three-member bloc formed between two investor-appointed directors and an independent chair. This bloc began steering the company towards an aggressive acquisition strategy that suited their own portfolios but strained the firm's cash position. By the time the CEO recognised the depth of their alignment, the momentum was too strong to reverse without risking a public rift. In contrast, a hardware start-up navigating a contentious down-round secured a more balanced outcome when the founder identified a quiet but influential director with relationships in both the investor and independent camps. By equipping this director with detailed scenario modelling ahead of the vote, the founder enabled them to act as a mediator, softening hardline positions and preserving board unity.

Philosophically, the presence of politics on a board is not inherently corrosive. Politics, in its purest sense, is the process by which groups with differing interests arrive at collective decisions. The danger lies in allowing these politics to operate unchecked, unacknowledged, and unmanaged. *A founder who treats political dynamics as beneath their notice risks becoming a passenger in their own company's governance.* By contrast, a founder who approaches them with clear-eyed realism can channel them towards productive ends—turning rivalries into intellectual competition, alliances into engines of execution, and even hidden agendas into aligned incentives where possible.

Ultimately, the ability to recognise and manage board politics is less about mastering manipulation and more about sustaining agency. It is about ensuring that the most important decisions are shaped by deliberate strategy rather than by the gravitational pull of unseen forces. In the high-stakes environment of a growth company, that distinction can mean the difference between a board that challenges and supports in equal measure, and one that quietly erodes a founder's influence until it is gone entirely.

Chapter 9
Exit Planning from Day One

For many founders, the very word "exit" carries a quiet unease—connotations of surrender, of moving on, or of betraying the mission that sparked the company's creation. This reaction is understandable, yet fundamentally misreads the nature of an exit. It is not an ending in the literary sense, where the final chapter closes and the story ceases. Rather, it is a pivotal scene that reshapes the narrative, influencing how the venture will be remembered and how it will endure beyond its original architect. To consider an exit from the earliest days is not to admit finite ambition; it is to practise strategic foresight. Every investor, every executive, and every founder will, inevitably, part ways with the enterprise in its current form. Ignoring that reality risks leaving the most consequential stage of the company's life to chance.

Early planning for an exit is less about pinpointing the exact mechanics of a future transaction than it is about cultivating optionality. A founder who maintains a clear view of possible outcomes—trade sale, IPO, secondary buyout, or strategic merger—makes choices differently regarding capital structure, governance, product positioning, and market expansion. These decisions accumulate into a trajectory that either widens the field of future possibilities or gradually constrains it, often invisibly. A company built without regard for what future acquirers or public markets value may, years later, operate successfully yet fail to meet the criteria for premium valuations.

Consider two otherwise promising companies in the same sector. One dismisses exit discussions as premature distractions, focusing solely on product development and near-term growth. The other, equally committed to customer value, quietly maps potential acquirers, observes comparable IPOs, and nurtures investor relationships with a future liquidity event in mind. When the market shifts—through regulatory changes, consolidation among competitors, or sudden investor appetite—the second company does not scramble to retrofit its structure; it steps through a door that has been carefully prepared for years.

A founder's personal horizon is often the least examined factor. The romantic image of a founder remaining at the helm for decades is increasingly rare in high-growth sectors, where timing, scale, and capital dynamics frequently necessitate an earlier transition. Yet the question of when to exit, and in what capacity to remain involved, is not purely financial. Burnout, shifting personal priorities, a desire to launch new ventures, or the recognition that a different leadership profile suits the next phase all inform the optimal moment to step aside. Founders who neglect this introspection risk clinging too long, eroding momentum, or exiting hastily, foregoing the opportunity to shape the terms of their departure.

Investor expectations add further complexity. Venture funds, for instance, operate within finite lifespans, often seeking liquidity within a decade to return capital to their own limited partners. A founder building for twenty years must reconcile that horizon with backers' potential impatience. Misalignment here is not a minor annoyance; it can fracture relationships and unravel strategic cohesion. Disciplined founders assess each investor's return profile and liquidity preferences before capital is accepted, avoiding later conflicts where conviction and financial pressure collide.

Reverse-engineering an exit blends art and science. It requires identifying what potential buyers, public markets, or strategic partners value most—recurring revenue, defensible intellectual property, geographic reach, market share—and deliberately sequencing growth milestones to enhance these attributes. This does not mean transforming the business into something it is not; it means amplifying the qualities that will render it irresistible to the right buyer at the right moment. Practically, this may involve pacing international expansion to demonstrate dominance in one region before replicating the model elsewhere, rather than scattering resources thinly in pursuit of superficial reach.

Paradoxically, the companies best positioned for an exit are often the least desperate to pursue one. By aligning operational excellence with market desirability from inception, founders create enterprises that could remain independent indefinitely yet remain consistently attractive to strategic suitors. This stance is not merely hedging; it is power. The founder negotiates from a position of genuine choice, able to decline offers that do not meet their criteria without compromising the company's trajectory.

This chapter invites a reframing: to perceive exit planning not as a distraction from the present, but as a lens through which today's decisions are sharpened. It challenges the notion that focus on an exit signals diminished commitment, positioning it instead as a form of stewardship. Readers will explore how personal goals, investor timelines, and market realities intersect to preserve—or erode—control over perhaps the most consequential decision a founder will ever make. Deliberate milestone design transforms an abstract future event into a navigable pathway, one in which value, timing, and strategic freedom are maximised rather than left to chance. The exit is not the epilogue; it is the moment when authorship of the venture is most fully tested.

Exits Are Not Endings: Why thinking about exit strategy early shapes better growth decisions

The most resilient companies are often those whose founders thought about their departure long before anyone imagined it would happen. This truth runs counter to the romanticised narrative of entrepreneurship, where commitment is measured in decades at the helm and any hint of an exit is seen as a betrayal of purpose. Yet the evidence is overwhelming: *the sooner a founder acknowledges that every business relationship—whether with investors, employees, or markets—has a natural horizon, the more intelligently they can design for growth.* The point of early exit thinking is not to accelerate departure; it is to ensure that the path you take towards expansion leads somewhere worth arriving at.

An exit is not the equivalent of closing the doors or switching off the lights—it is a transformation of ownership, control, or structure that can, when executed well, unlock resources, strategic partnerships, and scale beyond the reach of the original entity. The problem is that too many founders conflate "exit" with "ending", treating it as a future problem to be addressed only when circumstances force their hand. By that point, the flexibility to shape the event in one's favour is usually diminished. Without intentional early planning, the timing and terms of the exit are dictated by external pressures—an investor's fund life, a market downturn, or an opportunistic acquisition offer—rather than by the company's own readiness and objectives.

Consider the case of a fast-growing consumer technology company with impressive user adoption but minimal thought given to capital structure or acquisition desirability. The founder's focus is entirely on product innovation and brand building, which in itself is admirable. But when a strategic buyer emerges, eager to consolidate market share, the company's fragmented cap table, incomplete intellectual property assignments, and lack of contractual revenue streams erode the acquisition price and introduce deal uncertainty. By contrast, a peer company that has been built with an awareness of potential exit pathways—securing clean IP ownership, locking in key revenue agreements, and establishing governance systems trusted by acquirers—will find itself in a far stronger position to negotiate. The disparity in outcomes here is not a reflection of operational quality, but of structural foresight.

Early exit planning reframes how growth decisions are made. Product roadmaps are not only evaluated for customer impact but also for how they influence valuation drivers. Expansion strategies are assessed not just for market penetration, but for alignment with the interests of potential acquirers or public market investors. Even decisions about leadership hires shift in character—where a founder might once have prioritised a visionary with experimental instincts, they might instead balance that with an operator who understands the metrics, compliance standards, and strategic narratives that make a business credible to outside buyers. *The discipline is in recognising that building for a sustainable future and building for an attractive exit are not mutually exclusive; in many cases, they are the same project approached with greater clarity.*

Some founders fear that thinking about an exit too early will undermine their commitment to the mission, or signal to their team that they are "building to sell" rather than "building to last". This is a false dichotomy. The companies most attractive to acquirers or public investors are almost always those delivering exceptional value to their customers and operating with financial discipline. A deliberate exit strategy does not require distorting the mission—it requires making choices that keep strategic options open. The art is in *designing the business so that remaining independent is viable, but being acquired is effortless should the right opportunity arise.*

There is also a psychological advantage in this approach. By confronting the inevitability of transition, a founder removes the emotional volatility that can cloud judgment when unsolicited offers arrive or market conditions shift. Too often, founders are seduced by flattering acquisition overtures only to realise, too late, that the timing undermines value or leaves critical work unfinished. Conversely, some reject offers out of misplaced sentiment, not recognising that waiting another two or three years will expose the company to risks—technological disruption, regulatory change, capital scarcity—that could reduce its attractiveness or even its survival prospects.

One of the most underappreciated aspects of early exit thinking is the role it plays in aligning stakeholders. Investors, particularly institutional ones, operate on defined timelines for returning capital to their own backers. Employees may have stock options whose value depends entirely on a liquidity event. Strategic partners may invest resources in joint ventures on the assumption that the business will eventually be integrated into a larger entity. If these timelines and expectations are not discussed early, misalignment festers. The result is pressure building at inopportune moments, forcing exits on terms the founder might have avoided had they planned for them. Transparent early discussions about possible exit horizons, even in hypothetical terms, create a shared strategic frame of reference.

Importantly, early exit planning also helps to resist bad exits. A founder who knows the conditions under which they would accept a deal—valuation thresholds, cultural fit with the acquiring entity, treatment of employees, and post-deal involvement—can walk away from offers that fail those criteria without second-guessing themselves. They are not hostage to the allure of a windfall because they have defined in advance what constitutes a *good* outcome. This stance is not only protective; it signals to potential acquirers that the company has leverage, which often improves the quality of future offers.

If there is a philosophical pivot here, it is to see the exit not as a binary event that "happens" to a company, but as the culmination of a long sequence of decisions. Market leaders in various industries—whether in technology, manufacturing, or consumer goods—often appear to make opportunistic exits when conditions turn in their favour. Yet behind these moments lies years of deliberate positioning: securing the right regulatory approvals, building a defensible moat of intellectual property, cultivating strategic partnerships, and embedding performance metrics that resonate with buyers. Without this preparation, the same market conditions might have led to a lower valuation, a loss of negotiating control, or no deal at all.

The most telling evidence comes from founders who have exited more than once. Many will admit that their first exit was largely shaped by chance and reactive decision-making, but that their subsequent ventures were built with the endgame in mind from the outset. They choose investors whose time horizons and deal-making philosophies match their own, they structure employee incentives to align with potential transaction timelines, and they adopt reporting standards that will hold up under the due diligence of sophisticated acquirers. These are not cynical shortcuts—they are markers of maturity in building a business whose growth trajectory is coherent from first investment to final handover.

Ultimately, early exit strategy is less about a fixed plan than about cultivating adaptability. Markets shift, personal circumstances change, and opportunities appear unexpectedly. A founder who has been thinking in exit terms from day one can assess these changes not with panic or confusion, but with the clarity of someone who has already mapped the range of acceptable outcomes and the paths that lead there. They understand that the best exits—those that maximise value while preserving the company's core achievements—are rarely accidents. They are the product of sustained, intentional design. And in that sense, far from signalling the end of the story, the exit is the moment when the discipline of leadership is most fully expressed.

The Founder's Endgame: Personal and professional factors in deciding when—and how—to exit

Every founder faces a moment—whether anticipated or unplanned—when the question is no longer how to grow the business, but whether to continue leading it at all. The mythology of entrepreneurship often encourages the belief that this decision will be obvious, perhaps arriving with a sense of natural closure or perfect timing. In reality, exits are rarely so cleanly signposted. They are shaped by a complex interplay of personal ambitions, professional obligations, market forces, and the shifting identities of both the founder and the company. *A successful endgame is not just the sale of a business or a public listing—it is the culmination of a founder's capacity to align their personal values, financial needs, and leadership legacy with the structural realities of their venture.*

For many founders, the business is more than a commercial undertaking; it is an extension of their identity. The early years are marked by intense personal sacrifice and an all-encompassing sense of ownership. This deep identification with the company can make the idea of stepping away feel like an act of self-erasure. Yet the qualities that make a founder effective in the early, improvisational phases of growth are not always the same ones needed to run a mature organisation. Recognising this shift is not an admission of weakness; it is an acknowledgement of the natural lifecycle of leadership. Staying too long out of sentiment can be as damaging as leaving too early out of fear.

Personal readiness is often underestimated in exit planning. Financial independence is only one dimension—sometimes not even the most important one. A founder may achieve substantial wealth from an exit yet feel unmoored without the daily purpose, status, and community that the business provided. Others, exhausted by years of unrelenting pressure, may find that their decision to sell is driven less by market timing than by a desire to reclaim health, relationships, or creative energy. *The best founders approach the endgame with the same intentionality they brought to starting the business—seeing it not as an ending to be endured, but as a deliberate choice about how to live the next chapter of their lives.*

Professional considerations carry their own weight. No founder operates in isolation; they are bound to investors, employees, customers, and strategic partners whose fortunes may be directly tied to the exit. Timing, therefore, cannot be dictated solely by personal preference. A venture-backed founder, for example, must navigate investor liquidity timelines. Private equity funds have finite lives, and their pressure for returns may not coincide with the founder's sense of the company's optimal trajectory. In other cases, a founder may have a duty to deliver stability for employees—choosing an acquirer that offers cultural alignment and career continuity even if it means accepting a lower valuation.

The health of the market exerts a decisive influence. A strong economy and favourable industry conditions can make an exit seem compelling, but they can also tempt founders into chasing inflated valuations, risking overextension in the hope of squeezing out a marginally better deal. Conversely, a founder in a down market faces the challenge of deciding whether to sell at a discount or to hold on through uncertain conditions. Here, discipline matters: understanding the company's resilience, competitive position, and cash reserves can distinguish a strategic hold from an emotional refusal to let go.

There is also the question of *how* to exit. Selling to a strategic acquirer can deliver immediate liquidity and integration into a larger platform, but it may involve relinquishing control over the brand's future. A private equity buyout can preserve independence in operations while providing capital for growth, though it often comes with aggressive performance expectations. An initial public offering offers prestige and access to deep capital markets, yet it transforms the founder into a public figure accountable to a broader set of stakeholders. Each pathway demands a different level of involvement post-transaction, and a founder must decide whether they wish to remain operationally engaged, serve in an advisory capacity, or step away entirely.

Examples abound of founders whose exit strategies were as much about personal philosophy as about economics. Some choose to leave at the peak, preserving the narrative of their success, even if they might have earned more by staying longer. Others intentionally sell to buyers who will continue their mission, prioritising legacy over valuation. Consider the founder of a mission-driven consumer brand who turned down multiple higher offers in favour of a buyer committed to ethical sourcing—a decision that may have baffled financial analysts but resonated deeply with employees and loyal customers. These decisions are not anomalies; they are the product of a clear endgame framework where money is only one measure of value.

The risk in avoiding endgame thinking is that the exit becomes reactive, dictated by exhaustion, investor pressure, or opportunistic offers rather than by strategic intent. Founders who delay these conversations with themselves often find they are making the most significant decision of their careers under suboptimal conditions. By contrast, those who define their personal and professional criteria early can evaluate opportunities with clarity, declining those that do not align and pursuing those that do without hesitation. *Clarity on the endgame is not a constraint—it is a filter that protects the founder's agency in moments of high stakes.*

Perhaps the most important shift for any founder is to see the endgame not as a loss of identity but as a continuation of influence in a new form. Many of the most successful serial entrepreneurs and investors channel the capital, networks, and experience from one exit into new ventures, philanthropic initiatives, or advisory roles that amplify their impact. In this sense, deciding when and how to exit is less about stepping away from relevance and more about redefining the arena in which one operates. The founder who plans their endgame with this perspective sees the exit not as a final act, but as a deliberate move in a longer strategic career.

In the end, the founder's endgame is a deeply personal calculus—one that blends ambition, responsibility, market realities, and the evolving sense of self. The most effective leaders understand that success is not only measured by what they build, but by *how and when they choose to let it go.* To master this decision is to recognise that leadership is finite, ownership is transient, and that the legacy of a founder is determined not just by the company they created, but by the wisdom with which they exited it.

Investor Exit Expectations: Aligning your timeline with your backers' liquidity needs

One of the most underappreciated truths in venture-backed companies is that the founder's desired exit timeline is rarely the only—or even the primary—clock that matters. Investors are not patient in perpetuity. They are bound by the structural realities of their own funds, fiduciary obligations to their limited partners, and the internal performance targets that determine whether they raise their next fund. *Your exit strategy, no matter how compelling on paper, must live in the same time zone as your investors' liquidity requirements—or friction, mistrust, and suboptimal deals are inevitable.*

At first glance, the objectives of founders and investors seem aligned: build a valuable company and realise a strong return. But while founders can, in theory, choose to run their company indefinitely, investors have an immutable expiry date. A typical venture capital or private equity fund has a lifespan of around ten years, sometimes with an option for limited extensions. Capital is drawn from limited partners, deployed into portfolio companies over the first few years, and then those positions must be exited—preferably with significant gains—before the fund closes. This fixed horizon means that a portfolio company acquired in year four is often expected to exit somewhere between years seven and nine of the fund, regardless of whether the founder believes the business has another five years of high growth ahead.

This dynamic is not inherently adversarial; it is simply the economic architecture of professional investing. Yet founders who fail to map their growth trajectory to the underlying constraints of their investors' capital will eventually feel the pressure. A company growing at a healthy but unspectacular rate may suddenly find itself pushed towards a sale or IPO not because the business is underperforming, but because the fund's clock is running out. Conversely, investors might resist a perfectly timed acquisition offer in the early years if they believe the valuation could be dramatically higher closer to their planned exit window.

One of the most practical yet overlooked steps in founder–investor alignment is understanding *exactly where you sit* in your investors' fund cycle. This is more than a passing question during due diligence—it should be an ongoing conversation. If your lead investor deployed capital from a fund that is already halfway through its life, the implicit expectation is that your company will generate liquidity sooner rather than later. If your capital comes from a newly raised fund, you may have more breathing room—but this is not a licence for complacency, as early wins can dramatically enhance an investor's track record and fund-raising momentum.

The tension between operational optimisation and liquidity timing becomes even more pronounced in multi-investor syndicates. Not all backers share the same timeframes or exit preferences. A corporate strategic investor may have no fixed fund life but a strong preference for acquisition-based exits that integrate the portfolio company into its own operations. A late-stage growth equity investor might prioritise a quick return through a public listing. Early-stage venture funds could be willing to wait, but only if the growth trajectory remains steep. In these scenarios, founders must become adept at expectation management—balancing the narrative so that each class of investor sees a credible path to their own definition of success.

One way to manage this complexity is to adopt a dual-lens approach to strategy: the *intrinsic value lens*—how the company is performing against its own operational potential—and the *liquidity lens*—how that performance intersects with investor timelines. These two perspectives are not always in sync. A founder may wish to invest heavily in R&D, delaying profitability to secure a defensible market position. From the intrinsic value perspective, this could be the optimal move. Through the liquidity lens, however, if the major investors' fund life is winding down, they may resist such a strategy, preferring to maximise short-term valuation to meet their return schedules. The founder who recognises this divergence early can negotiate a middle path—perhaps structuring partial liquidity events, secondary share sales, or staged exits that satisfy investor needs without derailing the company's long-term vision.

Case studies from both ends of the spectrum illustrate the stakes. There are founders who have rejected acquisition offers in the belief that patience would yield higher valuations, only to find their investors pushing for a sale years later under less favourable market conditions. Equally, there are founders who have been persuaded into earlier-than-desired exits, benefiting their investors but leaving personal ambitions unfulfilled. In both cases, the misalignment was not necessarily philosophical—it was chronological. The absence of early, explicit conversations about timelines allowed the pressure to surface only when decision-making had already become urgent.

The most effective founders treat investor exit expectations not as a constraint but as a design parameter for growth strategy. *By understanding the non-negotiable liquidity needs of their backers, they can reverse-engineer corporate milestones to align with those windows.* This could mean accelerating certain revenue streams, prioritising markets that deliver faster scale, or sequencing product launches to ensure that valuation inflection points occur within the investors' preferred horizon. It also means being transparent when internal realities diverge from original projections—giving investors the time to adjust expectations rather than presenting them with last-minute surprises.

There is also a reputational dimension. Investors are not one-time collaborators; their experience with you will shape how they speak about you to other capital providers, strategic partners, and the market at large. If you manage the exit process in a way that acknowledges and respects their timelines—even if compromises are necessary—you are more likely to be seen as a trustworthy operator, opening doors for future ventures. Founders who ignore these dynamics, on the other hand, risk being labelled as difficult, inflexible, or out of touch with capital market realities.

Ultimately, aligning with investor exit expectations is not about capitulating to external pressure. It is about integrating the structural logic of your backers' business model into your own strategic thinking. The founder who understands that every cheque comes with a clock attached is better equipped to set realistic milestones, negotiate from a position of awareness, and choose exit paths that honour both their vision and their investors' fiduciary imperatives. Liquidity, after all, is not just a financial outcome—it is a trust event. Meeting your investors' needs while safeguarding the integrity of your company's growth is one of the clearest signals that you are a leader who can deliver not only on the pitch, but on the promises that follow.

Reverse-Engineering Milestones: How to build toward an exit that maximises valuation and strategic options

The most successful exits are rarely the result of opportunistic timing or lucky market conditions; they are the product of deliberate, disciplined design. *Reverse-engineering an exit is not about predicting the exact day a deal will close—it is about constructing a growth path in which each milestone is an intentional step towards the valuation and strategic positioning you want buyers or public markets to see.* Without this structure, companies often arrive at the negotiation table with a good business but an incoherent story, forcing them to accept terms that reflect their current state rather than their true potential.

The process begins with a clear definition of the desired exit profile: the type of acquirer or market you aim to attract, the valuation range you seek, and the qualitative attributes that will make your company stand out in due diligence. This clarity is essential because different exit routes reward different strengths. A strategic acquirer may pay a premium for a defensible market niche, a unique technology, or customer relationships that fill a gap in their portfolio. A private equity buyer might value predictable recurring revenues, operational efficiency, and a management team that can execute post-acquisition integration. Public markets will scrutinise growth rates, addressable market size, and scalability far more than the nuances of a single product. Once this end-state is defined, you can work backwards to identify the financial, operational, and narrative milestones that will signal readiness to that specific audience.

Consider valuation multiples. They are not uniform across all companies; they are contextual, shaped by sector norms, market cycles, and investor appetite. If your target is a software-as-a-service exit at 10x ARR, and the sector median is 6x, you must design a growth and margin profile that justifies the premium. This could mean accelerating customer acquisition in high-retention segments, investing in a robust data analytics layer to create stickiness, or proving scalability through international expansion. The point is not just to hit revenue numbers but to structure the composition of that revenue so that it aligns with what your ideal acquirer values most. *It is the quality of the metrics, not just their magnitude, that shifts a negotiation from formulaic valuation to strategic premium.*

Reverse-engineering also demands an acute awareness of timing—not just in relation to your internal capabilities but in synchrony with market dynamics. If you are aiming for a sale to a consolidating industry player, you need to time your peak readiness with their acquisition cycle, which could be influenced by their own cash position, strategic pivots, or competitive pressures. For a public offering, you must consider market windows—periods when investor sentiment and comparable listings suggest a higher probability of a favourable reception. The founder who thinks five years ahead is not merely forecasting revenue; they are anticipating the macro conditions under which that revenue will be judged.

In practice, this approach requires constructing a milestone map with three layers: operational metrics, strategic proof points, and perception management. Operational metrics are the hard data—revenue, margins, user growth, retention, unit economics—that underpin valuation models. Strategic proof points are the less quantifiable but equally critical signals of market leadership: securing a marquee customer, winning industry awards, or landing a partnership with a dominant player in an adjacent market. Perception management is the art of shaping how the market, the media, and potential acquirers perceive your trajectory. This could involve thought leadership, strategic PR, or curated investor communications that reinforce your positioning without revealing proprietary details.

An overlooked aspect of reverse-engineering is the sequence in which milestones are achieved. The order matters because of how narratives are constructed. For example, launching in a new market before proving strong retention in your core market might dilute perceived focus. On the other hand, locking in high-profile clients before raising a growth round can create competitive tension among investors, boosting valuation ahead of your expansion phase. The sequencing should be choreographed so that each milestone amplifies the impact of the next, culminating in a compelling end-state story for the exit.

Real-world examples illustrate the point. A B2B payments company targeting acquisition by a global bank built its roadmap around three deliberate moves: securing regulatory approval in key jurisdictions, integrating with a major accounting software platform, and signing multi-year contracts with multinational clients. By the time negotiations began, the company's profile ticked every box the bank's acquisition committee prioritised, allowing it to command a valuation far above its raw revenue multiple. Conversely, a consumer-tech startup aiming for an IPO missed its optimal window because it chased user growth at the expense of profitability, leaving its S-1 filing vulnerable to scrutiny during a market correction. The misstep was not in ambition but in failing to reverse-engineer the path to a valuation profile resilient to changing investor sentiment.

Reverse-engineering also allows for contingency planning. Markets shift, competitors emerge, and regulatory landscapes change. When you understand the critical path to your desired exit, you can adapt without losing momentum. If a target acquirer is suddenly taken off the table due to their own M&A activity, you can pivot towards another class of buyers, knowing which proof points will resonate most with them. This agility is only possible when milestones are not arbitrary achievements but deliberate signals tied to a broader exit thesis.

The discipline extends to capital allocation. Every significant expenditure should be evaluated through the dual lens of operational necessity and exit signalling. Expanding into a low-margin product line might generate revenue but dilute your valuation multiple if it alters your positioning. Conversely, investing in a feature that improves unit economics or strengthens defensibility might yield a modest short-term return but pay off disproportionately in exit negotiations. The founder committed to a reverse-engineered path resists the temptation of vanity metrics or opportunistic detours that do not advance the exit narrative.

Crucially, reverse-engineering milestones is not a solitary exercise. It requires alignment across the leadership team, the board, and major investors. The roadmap must be explicit, with progress measured and adjusted at regular intervals. Without this shared visibility, internal priorities can drift—sales might chase volume over margin, marketing might optimise for awareness instead of conversion, and product might over-index on innovation at the expense of reliability. The milestone map acts as a unifying reference point, ensuring that all functions pull in the same direction towards the exit's strategic design.

Ultimately, the power of reverse-engineering lies in replacing reactive growth with intentional momentum. By beginning with the end in mind and working backwards, founders can transform an exit from a hopeful outcome into a managed event—one where valuation is maximised not by chance but by a sequence of deliberate, well-timed decisions that leave multiple strategic doors open when it matters most. In a market where timing, positioning, and proof points dictate leverage, *a founder without a reverse-engineered plan is negotiating from hope; a founder with one is negotiating from strength.*

Chapter 10
Surviving the Second Round (and the Third…)

The first fundraising round often carries an almost intoxicating sense of possibility. The company is new, the story fresh, and the air itself seems charged with the promise of untapped growth. But once the confetti settles, reality asserts itself: follow-on capital is an entirely different arena. By the second round—and every subsequent raise thereafter—the investor conversation shifts. No longer are hypotheticals sufficient; there is now a ledger of operational history, scrutinised line by line. The question becomes less "Could this work?" and more "Has it worked, and can it endure the strain of scaling?" It is here that founders begin to confront the delicate balance between disciplined persistence and the appearance of desperation.

A follow-on raise conducted under pressure demands a finely tuned strategy. Arriving at the market overextended—whether in headcount, commitments, or burn rate—signals a lack of control. Investors sense urgency instinctively, and urgency almost invariably depresses valuation. The founder who approaches the second or third round projecting strength, even in difficult circumstances, commands more negotiating leverage. This strength is not illusionary; it is forged through disciplined capital stewardship, measured growth targets, and a narrative that positions the raise as acceleration rather than rescue. The paradox is clear: the best way to secure funding under pressure is to avoid looking pressured at all.

Valuation discipline takes on even greater significance at this stage. The allure of inflating a first-round valuation is understandable—a higher paper value feels like a triumph. Yet if performance fails to match those numbers, subsequent rounds become traps. Down rounds carry more than financial consequences; they can erode trust, unsettle employees, and leave a permanent imprint on the company's investment history. Inflated valuations also skew decision-making, encouraging premature scaling, risky product expansions, and marketing sprees aimed at "justifying" the number rather than supporting sustainable growth. When reality collides with overoptimism, the correction is often harsh, and the founder's leverage in future rounds may be severely compromised.

Another force that emerges over multiple rounds is investor fatigue. Even loyal backers can disengage if the company stagnates or its trajectory no longer aligns with their portfolio priorities. Disinterest can manifest subtly: slower responses to emails, reduced participation in strategy discussions, or diminished willingness to champion the raise to new investors. Recognising these early signs is critical. Waiting until a relationship has fully cooled before re-engaging makes the climb steeper. Sometimes operational progress—delivering tangible results—rekindles enthusiasm. Other times, it is narrative: reframing the company's direction to align with evolving investor priorities. The objective is never to placate backers but to ensure they perceive the business as an ongoing opportunity, not a closed chapter.

A common misstep is treating later rounds as mere continuations of the first. Each raise is its own political, financial, and strategic event, shaped by shifting market conditions, competitor moves, and investor appetites. The charisma, vision, and early traction that carried the seed round must now be reinforced by evidence of execution, operational discipline, and adaptability. By this stage, the company is no longer a speculative "story stock"; it is a business with a track record that investors will interrogate as closely as the metrics themselves.

Consider a founder midway through a Series B raise when a major competitor launches a similar product at a lower price. The original fundraising narrative, focused on speed to scale, suddenly falters. Rather than stubbornly pushing forward, the team pivots—emphasising differentiation, defensibility, and strategic partnerships. Operational adjustments accompany the reframed pitch, attracting investors aligned with a longer-term competitive strategy rather than immediate market conquest. The lesson is clear: the raise that "changes everything" often does so because the founder adjusts both story and substance in real time, harmonising capital strategy with the evolving market.

Surviving follow-on rounds is as much about preserving optionality as it is about securing cash. The founder who raises without sacrificing control, without diluting excessively, and without becoming hostage to investor-driven growth paths retains the agility to navigate future opportunities and threats. This requires candid evaluation of trade-offs at every stage. A term sheet with a slightly lower valuation from a partner who shares your strategic vision can be far more valuable than a richer offer from an investor focused solely on short-term returns.

In the end, second, third, and all subsequent rounds are stress tests—not merely of the business model, but of a founder's ability to manage capital, relationships, and narrative under amplified scrutiny. Those who approach these raises as if they were the first often find themselves cornered. Those who evolve—recognising that each new round is a distinct negotiation—position themselves not just to survive but to shape the company's trajectory on their own terms. Each raise, then, becomes less about chasing capital and more about orchestrating the partnerships that sustain both vision and founder influence over time.

Raising Follow-On Capital Under Pressure: How to approach future rounds without looking desperate or overleveraged

The moment a founder enters the market for a follow-on round under visible strain, the rules of engagement change. Investors—especially institutional ones—are acutely sensitive to power dynamics in capital negotiations. If they detect you are backed into a corner, the conversation is no longer about shared vision; it becomes about terms extraction. Pressure distorts perception, and perception in fundraising is as potent as the numbers on your balance sheet. The challenge is that capital scarcity, competitive threats, or operational setbacks can force a founder back into the market sooner than planned. Under these conditions, success is not simply about convincing someone to write a cheque—it is about doing so while preserving your company's credibility, leverage, and long-term optionality.

The first principle in avoiding the stench of desperation is narrative control. Under pressure, founders often frame the raise reactively: "We need this to extend runway." That may be factually true, but it is rarely the story that inspires confidence. The story that resonates under duress is one that reframes necessity as opportunity: positioning the raise as fuel for a targeted strategic initiative that accelerates a well-defined growth vector. Even if liquidity is the underlying driver, the external presentation must tie the capital to momentum, not survival. This requires tight integration between operational planning and investor communications, ensuring that every element—product roadmap, sales pipeline, market expansion—reflects purposeful, forward-looking deployment of funds rather than a scramble to stay afloat.

The second principle is capital discipline. Overleveraging before a raise is one of the most avoidable mistakes founders make, and it becomes glaringly visible during diligence. Excessive debt, aggressive forward hiring without corresponding revenue, or high fixed costs relative to recurring income signal to investors that you are trading resilience for short-term optics. If your cost structure suggests fragility, even sympathetic investors will question your ability to withstand shocks. Maintaining a lean operational profile going into a pressured raise not only buys you time but also widens the pool of potential backers—some of whom will step away entirely if they sense structural overextension. Restraint is an asset in itself, as it signals that you have not allowed market pressures to dictate reckless growth.

Timing, too, plays an outsized role. Founders often wait until cash reserves are dangerously low before beginning the next raise, inadvertently putting themselves in the most unfavourable negotiating position possible. Under pressure, this creates a vicious cycle: compressed timelines lead to hurried due diligence, which leads to lower leverage in structuring terms. The disciplined founder raises earlier than strictly necessary, even at the cost of diluting slightly more than they would prefer, because they understand that an extra quarter of cash can mean the difference between a strategic capital partnership and a take-it-or-leave-it deal. The irony is that the less urgently you need capital, the more readily it is offered.

Real-world cases illustrate this dynamic vividly. One mid-stage SaaS company found itself with less than six months' runway after a failed market expansion. Instead of framing the raise as a rescue, the CEO focused the pitch on a proven, high-margin vertical they had neglected during the expansion push. They presented the capital request as the means to aggressively consolidate leadership in that niche, supported by fresh customer acquisition data from early re-entry into that market. By shifting the conversation from "we're recovering from a misstep" to "we're doubling down where we're already winning," they closed the round with terms that preserved founder equity and secured an investor syndicate better aligned with their refined focus. The underlying pressure never disappeared—it was simply reframed into a position of strategic intent.

Equally important is investor selection. Under pressure, founders often cast the widest possible net, engaging any fund or angel willing to take a meeting. This approach may create noise rather than traction. It is far more effective to narrow the target list to investors with both the capacity and inclination to move quickly, and whose portfolio composition suggests they understand your current stage and sector. Pressure raises are not the moment to educate a new investor on the fundamentals of your market; they are the moment to engage those who already grasp the thesis and can evaluate your opportunity without an elongated learning curve. Investors who see your raise as an extension of a strategic narrative they already buy into are far less likely to exploit the timing to drive punitive terms.

A less discussed but equally critical factor is signalling risk. In high-pressure situations, existing investors can either strengthen or weaken your hand. If they participate in the round—or even signal strong public support—it reassures new investors that insiders believe in the company's trajectory. If they abstain or appear lukewarm, it amplifies the perception of fragility. Founders should manage these optics deliberately, securing early commitments from key insiders before opening the raise more broadly. Sometimes this requires offering pro-rata protections or other small incentives to encourage participation, but the reputational payoff can be significant.

Managing investor perception under pressure is not purely about storytelling; it is also about operational proof. The ability to point to measurable, recent wins—whether in revenue, customer retention, product innovation, or strategic partnerships—can counteract the negative assumptions that arise when you return to the market sooner than expected. The wins do not need to be monumental, but they must be relevant and timely, signalling that momentum exists independent of the capital infusion. Without such proof points, even the best-crafted narrative risks sounding hollow.

Finally, there is the question of psychological posture. Founders under pressure often enter negotiations with a subtext of appeasement, eager to accept whatever terms are on offer to secure runway. This mindset is detectable and corrosive to negotiating power. The alternative is not arrogance, but calm resolve: the ability to communicate that while this capital would be strategically valuable, the company is not without other paths forward. Whether those alternatives are bridge financing, cost restructuring, or staged growth without new capital, the key is to enter the room with optionality—both real and perceived. The more you believe you have choices, the more convincingly you project stability.

Approaching a follow-on raise under pressure is an exercise in managing both the internal mechanics of the business and the external theatre of investor relations. The founder who can align disciplined operations, strategic storytelling, and targeted investor engagement will find that pressure need not equate to weakness. Indeed, in the hands of a prepared and self-aware leader, it can serve as the crucible in which the company's most compelling and investable narrative is forged.

Valuation vs. Reality: Avoiding inflated valuations that damage long-term prospects

A valuation is not a verdict; it is a narrative quantified. Yet too many founders treat it as a trophy—proof that their company is winning—rather than as a financial construct that must withstand scrutiny across multiple funding cycles. An inflated valuation can feel intoxicating in the short term: it generates headlines, signals momentum, and flatters the ego. But if it is not grounded in the company's actual performance, market conditions, and path to profitability, it becomes a trap—compressing future strategic options and loading the business with expectations it cannot meet. The damage is often invisible at first, emerging only in later rounds when performance lags the implied trajectory, investors reprice risk aggressively, and the founder's negotiating leverage evaporates.

The mechanics of the problem are straightforward but frequently underestimated. A valuation is, in theory, the price the market is willing to pay for a share of your future. If the future implied by that price does not materialise—because of slower growth, shifting markets, or operational missteps—the next funding event forces a reckoning. Down rounds not only dilute equity more severely but also erode confidence among employees, partners, and customers. Even when a founder manages to avoid an outright down round, they may be forced into flat valuations with punitive terms—liquidation preferences, ratchets, or governance concessions—that compromise control and economics for years. *A misaligned valuation is therefore not a number to celebrate, but a liability to manage.*

Consider the case of a consumer-tech startup that secured a $200 million valuation on the back of a single high-growth year fuelled by pandemic-induced demand. The founders believed the multiple would be justified as the trend continued. It didn't. When growth normalised, their revenue fell short of the projections embedded in the prior valuation by 40%. The next raise became a negotiation over how much of the company they would need to surrender to secure capital. The very investors who had championed the aggressive price in the previous round were now the ones insisting on aggressive downside protection. The founders' options narrowed: accept the terms or face a cash shortfall that would have made the company uninvestable.

This cycle repeats across sectors, often for the same reason: valuations are set not by intrinsic metrics alone but by market sentiment, competitive pressure, and the founder's own appetite for dilution. The temptation to push for the highest possible price is understandable—higher valuations preserve ownership in the short term and signal market leadership. But when the number exceeds the sustainable growth trajectory, it silently resets the baseline for all future discussions. Every investor in subsequent rounds will anchor their expectations to that inflated baseline, forcing the company to chase an artificial growth curve rather than the optimal strategic one. This is how valuations distort strategy: instead of allocating resources to durable product-market fit, founders overextend to hit arbitrary revenue targets in order to "grow into" the price.

A disciplined approach to valuation begins with intellectual honesty about the company's fundamentals. That means resisting the urge to benchmark solely against outlier deals in the sector, or to assume that a competitor's inflated raise validates your own push for a similar number. Context matters. An enterprise SaaS company with long-term contracts and high gross margins can justify a multiple that would be reckless for a hardware startup with capital-intensive operations and unpredictable sales cycles. This is not conservatism for its own sake—it is about *matching valuation to the risk profile* in a way that preserves credibility with future investors.

One of the most dangerous justifications for an inflated valuation is the belief that it can always be "grown into" before the next round. This assumes a level of predictability in markets that rarely exists, and it ignores the impact of macroeconomic shifts on funding appetites. In a tightening capital environment, even strong companies see valuation compression; for overvalued companies, the fall is steeper and more painful. The safer path is to negotiate for a fair, defensible price that aligns with both current performance and realistic near-term growth. This ensures that subsequent raises can be framed as building on steady momentum rather than clawing back from overreach.

The long-term implications go beyond financing mechanics. Valuation influences hiring strategy, partnership negotiations, and even acquisition outcomes. High paper valuations often translate into high expectations for employee stock options. If the exit fails to clear those expectations, the result is disillusionment and attrition among key talent. In M&A discussions, inflated valuations can cause acquirers to walk away or delay offers, waiting for a price correction they see as inevitable. In both cases, the founder's leverage is weakened not by a lack of opportunity but by an overhang of misaligned expectations.

The healthiest founder-investor relationships are built on transparency around valuation logic. Founders who proactively explain why they are targeting a particular price—grounding it in defensible metrics, market comparables, and realistic projections—tend to attract investors who are aligned on the long game. Those investors are more likely to support the company through inevitable fluctuations, because they bought into a rational growth story rather than a hype-driven multiple. This alignment is far harder to achieve if the price is inflated purely to maximise short-term optics.

There is also a cultural dimension to consider. In some ecosystems, notably in certain U.S. venture hubs, the "go big or go home" mentality creates a bias toward pushing valuations aggressively, on the theory that the upside justifies the risk. In others, such as many European markets, there is a stronger emphasis on sustainable growth and profitability, which tends to moderate valuation inflation. Founders operating in cross-border contexts must be especially aware of these cultural differences; raising a high-priced round in one market can create friction when courting investors from another with a more conservative lens.

In practice, avoiding valuation traps requires a combination of financial discipline, strategic foresight, and ego management. The founder must weigh the trade-off between near-term dilution and long-term flexibility, recognising that the cost of giving up a few extra points of equity now may be far lower than the cost of being boxed into a punitive future round. They must also be willing to challenge investors—politely but firmly—when pressured to accept a higher price than the business can justify. Saying no to flattering numbers is counterintuitive, but it is often the decision that protects the company's strategic integrity.

Ultimately, valuation should be treated not as a peak to summit but as a pace to set. The goal is not to impress the market for a quarter but to maintain a trajectory that can be sustained across multiple stages of growth, each building on the last without the distortions of artificial inflation. In doing so, founders preserve their most valuable currency: the ability to choose their investors, dictate their strategic path, and raise capital on terms that strengthen rather than weaken the company's long-term prospects.

Investor Fatigue: Recognising when backers are losing interest and how to re-engage them

The relationship between a founder and their investors is often framed in transactional terms—capital for equity, performance for returns—but beneath the formal agreements lies an ongoing human dynamic that can make or break a company's trajectory. Investors, like founders, are subject to shifting priorities, opportunity costs, and emotional engagement. They enter with enthusiasm, commit resources, and invest social capital in championing the business. Yet over time, that energy can wane. The warning signs of investor fatigue are subtle at first: less responsiveness to updates, reduced attendance at key meetings, fewer introductions to potential partners. Left unchecked, this drift can solidify into disinterest, depriving the company not just of fresh capital but of the advocacy and support that often matter more than the money itself. Recognising and addressing this shift early is one of the most underappreciated skills in the founder's toolkit.

Investor fatigue is not always a reflection of poor performance. In some cases, it emerges from portfolio dynamics. Venture funds have finite bandwidth; once they've allocated the bulk of their investment to a company, they may shift focus to earlier-stage bets or higher-growth portfolio stars. Sometimes the cause is external: a market downturn that reorients the fund's priorities, or an internal change in leadership that alters investment theses. Founders often take this personally, but the truth is that investor attention is a scarce resource, and even promising businesses can find themselves competing for it. *The challenge is to distinguish between temporary distraction and a deeper loss of conviction.*

A telling pattern is when investors stop initiating contact or providing unsolicited input. In the early stages, engaged backers will often send industry articles, competitive intelligence, or talent referrals without being asked. When that stops, it's rarely accidental. Another indicator is when they begin hedging their language in conversations about future funding—subtly shifting from "when you raise the next round" to "if you raise the next round." These linguistic cues matter, because they signal an adjustment in their mental model of the company's prospects. Ignoring them risks walking blind into a funding gap.

The temptation for founders is to overcorrect by bombarding investors with positive updates in an attempt to rekindle excitement. While transparency and momentum are essential, desperation is counterproductive. The most effective re-engagement strategy is not to flood inboxes with marginal wins, but to demonstrate strategic clarity. Investors want to see a credible path forward, not noise. If metrics have plateaued, acknowledge it directly, articulate the specific levers you're pulling to break through, and show evidence of progress—even if early. The credibility gained by owning the narrative often outweighs the discomfort of admitting a slowdown.

In some cases, the right move is to reframe the relationship entirely. An investor who has mentally exited the deal may still provide value in non-financial ways—introductions, market intelligence, or credibility by association—if approached with specific, low-friction asks. The key is to make those asks targeted and actionable. A vague "We'd appreciate any connections you can make" is easy to ignore; a precise "Can you introduce us to the VP of Partnerships at Company X?" is far more likely to get a response. Investors with fading interest are unlikely to commit to large ongoing efforts, but they may still contribute in ways that require minimal time or decision-making energy.

There is also a preventive dimension to this problem. Founders who treat investor relations as an ongoing discipline—rather than a flurry of activity around funding rounds—are less likely to face acute disengagement. That means establishing a predictable rhythm of communication, one that balances transparency with respect for their time. Quarterly deep dives into metrics and strategy, supplemented by concise interim updates, keep the relationship alive without creating fatigue. Just as importantly, those updates should not read like investor marketing collateral; they should convey the genuine state of the business, including the challenges. Paradoxically, this builds trust and keeps investors emotionally invested, because they feel part of solving the problems rather than spectators to a managed narrative.

There will be times when re-engagement is neither possible nor worth pursuing. Some investors simply decide—whether through portfolio strategy or personal bias—that a company no longer fits their objectives. In these cases, founders must avoid the trap of devoting excessive time to winning back a lost audience at the expense of running the business. Recognising when to shift focus toward cultivating new investor relationships is part of preserving strategic bandwidth. The founder's role is not to convert every wavering backer into a believer, but to ensure the company's momentum is sustained with or without their active support.

Still, there is a compelling case for making the effort before writing an investor off. Engagement can be rekindled through well-timed strategic inflection points: a product pivot that opens a new market, the signing of a transformative customer, or a shift in macro conditions that suddenly validates the company's thesis. These moments have disproportionate signalling power. If communicated effectively, they can reset the investor's mental model and reignite interest. The critical word is "effectively." A perfunctory email will not suffice; the update should be framed in a way that connects the development directly to the investor's original reasons for backing the company, reminding them why they saw potential in the first place.

Founders also need to be alert to their own role in causing fatigue. Investors disengage more quickly when they sense strategic drift, opaque decision-making, or defensive responses to hard questions. Over time, these patterns erode trust and make backers less inclined to commit further resources. Conversely, even in tough markets, a founder who projects competence, adaptability, and decisiveness will hold investor attention longer. This is not about projecting unearned confidence; it is about showing that the company is led by someone who is making conscious, data-driven decisions rather than reacting impulsively to circumstances.

Ultimately, managing investor fatigue is about protecting optionality. An investor who remains engaged—even passively—is far easier to re-activate for bridge funding, strategic introductions, or signalling support in future rounds than one who has mentally checked out. By recognising early warning signs, responding with strategic clarity, and sustaining a baseline of trust, founders can avoid the abrupt shocks that come from discovering too late that their backers have quietly moved on. The goal is not to keep every investor equally energised at all times—that is neither realistic nor necessary—but to ensure that no relationship with potential long-term value is allowed to decay through neglect or misreading of signals.

Case Study: The Round That Changed Everything: Lessons from a startup that pivoted mid-raise to secure the right investors

It is tempting to view fundraising as a linear process: a company defines its strategy, builds a deck, approaches investors, negotiates terms, and closes the round. In reality, for many startups, the process is messier, more iterative, and at times brutally unpredictable. The case of Luminor Analytics—a data intelligence startup that entered its Series B raise with high ambitions only to pivot mid-process—offers a rare, instructive look into what happens when market conditions, investor expectations, and company strategy collide. The outcome not only saved the company but reshaped its trajectory, validating a new business model and attracting a stronger calibre of investor than it had originally targeted.

When Luminor began its Series B roadshow, it was riding a wave of early success. Its AI-driven analytics platform for retail operations had gained solid traction among mid-market clients in Europe, and its Series A investors were keen for it to expand aggressively into the United States. The pitch was simple: raise £25 million to build a US sales force, scale infrastructure, and outpace competitors in a growing sector. Initial investor meetings were encouraging; the technology was credible, the founding team was respected, and the retail analytics market was buoyed by a post-pandemic surge in e-commerce. Yet by the end of the first quarter of pitching, interest had cooled. Term sheets were slow to materialise, and the valuations offered were far below the founder's expectations.

The problem, as became clear in investor feedback, was not the product but the market segment. Several VCs questioned whether the retail sector was as defensible or scalable as Luminor claimed, noting that consumer spending patterns were becoming more volatile and that mid-market clients were less likely to weather downturns without slashing SaaS spending. Compounding this, two well-funded US competitors had emerged with similar offerings but a sharper enterprise focus, making Luminor's proposed expansion look riskier. The founder, Sarah Khan, faced a choice: push ahead with the original plan, accept a lower valuation and potentially misaligned investors, or rethink the strategy entirely.

What happened next is where most founders would have doubled down, determined to 'sell harder.' Khan took the opposite approach. Rather than treating investor hesitation as an obstacle to overcome, she treated it as market intelligence. Her leadership team paused the raise, ran a two-week sprint to reassess their total addressable market, and interviewed not just current clients but also prospects who had declined to buy. The insight was stark: while mid-market retailers were attracted to Luminor's solution, the enterprise segment—particularly multinational grocery and apparel chains—had pain points that Luminor's AI could address with only moderate product adjustments. Moreover, these enterprises had significantly higher switching costs and budgets that could sustain multi-year contracts.

Pivoting mid-raise is often seen as a sign of weakness, yet here it became a strategic advantage. Armed with a refined enterprise-first pitch, Luminor returned to the market, this time targeting a different set of investors—those with deep networks in enterprise software and retail supply chains. The raise goal was reduced to £18 million, with a heavier allocation for product customisation and less emphasis on an immediate US expansion. By aligning the capital ask with a sharper, more credible growth plan, the company not only secured commitments more quickly but attracted backers with sector expertise that proved critical in the subsequent scaling phase.

One of the most instructive elements of this case is how Khan managed the messaging to her existing investors. Admitting a mid-raise pivot can easily erode confidence, especially when prior funding was predicated on the original growth narrative. She avoided this pitfall by framing the pivot as an evolution rather than a retreat, demonstrating that the decision was data-driven, not reactive. The update deck did not shy away from the risks but showed in granular detail how the enterprise pivot could deliver higher gross margins, lower churn, and stronger defensibility. This candour preserved trust and even prompted one existing investor to increase their follow-on commitment. *The lesson here is that investors are far more willing to back a pivot when it is presented as the result of disciplined strategic thinking rather than desperation.*

The post-raise outcomes further underscore the long-term impact of the pivot. Within twelve months, Luminor closed three major enterprise contracts worth more than its entire mid-market annual recurring revenue. Its lead Series B investor, a global fund with significant enterprise SaaS holdings, was instrumental in securing introductions to decision-makers at these accounts. This was not accidental; by recalibrating both the investor target list and the strategic narrative, Luminor ensured that its new backers brought more than capital—they brought the relational capital and sector credibility to make the pivot viable.

There are, of course, risks in pivoting mid-raise. Had the product not been adaptable to enterprise needs without a costly rebuild, or had the leadership team lacked credibility in the eyes of new investors, the shift could have backfired. Furthermore, the timing was critical; delaying too long would have depleted cash reserves, reducing leverage in negotiations. The success of Luminor's pivot was partly due to the fact that it acted early, before the company's runway became a source of investor concern. This preserved optionality and avoided the perception of a distressed raise—a perception that can be fatal in competitive funding environments.

Founders can draw several durable insights from this episode. First, investor pushback—when it is consistent and grounded—should be interrogated, not dismissed. It is often an early signal of market perception that will be even harder to overcome post-investment. Second, aligning the investor base with the revised strategy is not optional. A pivot that delivers on paper but is supported by investors without relevant networks or conviction in the new direction risks becoming a hollow victory. Finally, speed and decisiveness matter. The longer a company straddles two narratives, the more both investors and employees begin to question its leadership.

Perhaps the most powerful takeaway from Luminor's experience is that the round that "changed everything" did so not because of the capital secured, but because it forced the company to clarify its strategic identity. By the time the raise closed, the business was not merely better funded—it was better positioned, better supported, and better understood by its stakeholders. For founders, the implication is clear: the fundraising process is not just a means of acquiring resources; it is a crucible in which the most enduring strategic decisions are often forged. The willingness to adapt those decisions under pressure can mark the difference between a raise that sustains you and a raise that transforms you.

Chapter 11
The Founder's Psychological Resilience Plan

The mythology of entrepreneurship has always been more alluring in concept than lived reality. Publicly, the founder is cast as a figure of unwavering vision and control—decisive in meetings, magnetic to investors, seemingly impervious to the strains felt by the team. Privately, the narrative is rarely so polished. Many founders discover that the period following a successful funding round—the very milestone once imagined as a relief—often brings a new, more complex set of pressures. Capital sits in the bank, yes, but so does expectation, amplified. Investors demand speed. Teams seek clarity. Competitors, now conscious of your resources, adjust their tactics. The founder realises that success is less a finish line and more the gateway to a harsher, more relentless race.

The loneliness of leadership in such circumstances is not physical but cognitive. The stakes rise, and fewer people within the organisation can genuinely share the burden of decision-making. Subordinates may be supportive, yet their dependence limits the extent of transparency. Investors are stakeholders, not confidants; their concern lies with outcomes, not with preserving the founder's mental equilibrium. Even co-founders may experience pressures asynchronously. This structural solitude transforms the founder's inner life into a central arena of business performance—rarely addressed in boardrooms, yet profoundly shaping the quality of every strategic decision.

In this context, stress is not merely an unfortunate by-product of leadership; it is a strategic variable. It colours cognitive clarity, interpersonal judgement, and risk appetite. Founders who learn to regulate stress gain an edge over peers equally skilled in execution but less adept at managing internal pressures. Regulation here is not denial, nor the pursuit of a stress-free existence—impossible and arguably undesirable—but an adaptive relationship with pressure: recognising when heightened arousal sharpens focus and when it begins to constrict perspective dangerously. Awareness of one's triggers, physiological responses, and recovery needs becomes as critical as interpreting a balance sheet. Without this mastery, the business will eventually manage the founder, not the other way around.

The value of a robust support network grows ever clearer in this light. The term has been diluted to mean any loosely affiliated acquaintances or online contacts, yet effective networks are deliberate constructs, built on trust, expertise, and relevance. Peers matter only if they share unvarnished truths about their own setbacks as well as successes. Mentors are effective when they challenge thinking without undermining confidence. Advisors contribute by offering insights inaccessible within the founder's immediate environment. The right network functions both as ballast and sail—stabilising the leader amid turbulence while guiding towards sounder decisions.

Burnout, the silent saboteur, seldom announces itself with a dramatic collapse. More often it creeps in insidiously: shorter temper, waning creativity, subtle erosion of empathy. Early recognition is critical. Signs vary: for some, the abandonment of exercise; for others, avoidance of difficult conversations; for yet others, sleeplessness despite exhaustion. Recovery must be intentional, not reactive. Such practices are not indulgences reserved for crisis but pre-emptive investments in sustained high performance. Waiting until burnout manifests is to operate in salvage mode rather than strategy mode.

This chapter reframes these realities, equipping founders to regard psychological resilience as a core business asset rather than a personal afterthought. It advocates a shift from passive endurance—simply "toughing it out"—to a proactive model integrating emotional stamina, adaptive stress management, high-value networks, and structured recovery into the fabric of leadership. These are not mere soft skills; they are determinants of whether post-funding growth is sustainable or precarious. By applying the same rigour to psychological resilience as to financial modelling or market analysis, founders can transform what is often their most vulnerable dimension into one of their most enduring competitive advantages.

The Loneliness of Leadership: Understanding the emotional toll of post-funding leadership

The moment a founder closes a significant funding round is often painted as the point where the wind shifts in their favour. The capital has arrived, the company's runway extends, and long-postponed plans can finally move forward. Yet for many founders, this is precisely the moment when a new, more isolating chapter begins. The emotional toll of post-funding leadership does not arise because the mission has changed, but because the role itself transforms in subtle but decisive ways. The founder is no longer the underdog pleading for oxygen; they are now the steward of other people's money, a figure onto whom investors, employees, and even customers project heightened expectations. This shift creates an invisible distance—a separation from those around them—that can feel both inevitable and disorienting.

The isolation is rarely about physical solitude. A funded founder is typically surrounded by more people than ever before: expanded teams, more frequent board meetings, higher-profile partnerships. Yet proximity is not the same as connection. The team looks to the founder for certainty, not vulnerability; their faith in leadership is tied to the perception of unwavering confidence. Investors, however supportive, remain bound by the fact that they have a financial stake to protect, which complicates the space for raw candour. Even among co-founders, experiences may diverge. One may feel energised by the spotlight, while another shoulders the emotional weight of decisions in a way that cannot be equally distributed. The result is a paradox: the more successful the company appears externally, the less room there is internally for the founder to express uncertainty without consequence.

The stakes of this loneliness are not abstract. Emotional isolation corrodes judgement. Without trusted counterparts to challenge assumptions or sanity-check instincts, the founder's decision-making risks becoming a closed loop—fed by their own fears, overconfidence, or misread signals. History offers examples of high-profile founders who made dramatic strategic missteps after surrounding themselves only with voices that echoed their own, not necessarily because they craved flattery, but because they lacked a safe channel for dissent. This is one of the under-acknowledged dangers of post-funding leadership: the structural incentives that make it harder to invite, or even tolerate, unfiltered feedback.

Moreover, the nature of the decisions a post-funding founder faces deepens this isolation. Pre-funding choices often revolve around survival—scrappy tactics, incremental wins, the pursuit of validation. Post-funding, the decisions expand in scale and consequence. Whether to accelerate headcount, pursue an acquisition, enter a new market, or adjust the product roadmap—these are calls that can alter the trajectory of the company irreversibly. The psychological pressure of knowing that a wrong move can erode not just capital but credibility magnifies the emotional load. When the founder cannot share that pressure openly, it calcifies into stress patterns that impact their leadership tone, their ability to inspire, and even their physical health.

Some founders respond by attempting to mask the strain, adopting a persona of perpetual control. While this may work in the short term, it comes at the cost of authenticity, which teams eventually detect. Employees tend to be far more perceptive than leaders imagine; they read subtle cues in behaviour and tone. A leader who insists on presenting only a perfectly polished front can inadvertently create a culture where others also hide difficulties, reducing the organisation's resilience. Conversely, founders who swing too far towards transparency—sharing every fear and doubt without filtration—can unintentionally destabilise confidence. The art lies in striking a balance: *selective vulnerability*, where honesty is paired with context and direction, so the team understands both the challenge and the plan to address it.

The emotional toll is compounded by the founder's own identity investment in the business. For many, the company is not just a professional pursuit but an extension of the self—its success or failure is experienced as deeply personal. Post-funding, this identification intensifies because external validation has been received in the form of capital. The implicit message is: *You were right, and now you must prove it at scale.* This dynamic makes it harder for founders to separate their sense of worth from the company's performance. A dip in metrics can feel like a personal indictment;

investor dissatisfaction can feel like a critique of their character rather than their strategy. Without mechanisms to maintain perspective, the founder risks conflating operational challenges with existential threats.

Real-world examples underscore the pattern. Consider the case of a health-tech founder who, after closing a sizeable Series B, found herself suddenly excluded from the informal camaraderie she had once enjoyed with her small team. With the influx of funds came new hires, many of whom joined expecting a fast-moving, well-resourced organisation—not a collaborative scrappy startup. The founder's previous role as an all-hands problem-solver evolved into one of strategic delegation, board presentations, and constant external engagement. She reported that, despite having more people in the building than ever, she felt "like the only person in the room without a peer." Without deliberate steps to build external sounding boards, she risked making decisions in a vacuum, driven by a blend of urgency and unprocessed stress.

There are, of course, counterexamples—leaders who maintain deep connection despite the constraints. These founders often share common habits: they invest early in peer networks outside the company, cultivate at least one trusted confidant who has no financial stake in the business, and consciously create spaces where genuine dialogue can occur without immediate consequences. They also resist the temptation to use the role as a shield, allowing themselves moments of unfiltered humanity without undermining the authority the position demands. Such strategies do not erase the inherent solitude of post-funding leadership, but they do prevent it from becoming corrosive.

Ultimately, *the loneliness of leadership is not a flaw in the founder's character but a structural condition of the role.* Understanding its mechanics is the first step towards managing it. By recognising that isolation will intensify after funding—and by designing intentional counterweights in advance—founders can avoid the subtle slide into emotional detachment that so often precedes poor strategic judgement. The ability to lead well post-funding is not simply a function of intellect, vision, or capital—it is equally dependent on the capacity to remain connected, grounded, and emotionally resourced in the face of expectations that grow faster than the company itself.

Stress as a Strategic Variable: Techniques for managing stress to preserve decision-making clarity

In high-stakes leadership, stress is not merely an unavoidable by-product of responsibility—it is a dynamic force that can be channelled or allowed to corrode. Many founders instinctively regard stress as something to be eliminated, treating it as a contaminant to be purged before "real" thinking can happen. This view is both naïve and operationally dangerous. The reality is that stress, like capital, is a resource. It can be squandered through mismanagement or harnessed as a driver of focus, urgency, and creativity. The most effective leaders do not seek to banish stress entirely; they learn to calibrate it, recognising that their ability to make sound, high-impact decisions under pressure often depends less on the absence of stress than on their mastery over its effects.

Understanding stress as a strategic variable begins with acknowledging its dual nature. Physiologically, stress primes the body to respond to threat—narrowing attention, sharpening reaction time, and mobilising energy. These mechanisms are adaptive in situations requiring immediate action, such as closing a critical deal or responding to an unexpected operational failure. Yet the same responses become maladaptive when the pressure is chronic and diffuse. Sustained high cortisol levels degrade cognitive flexibility, impair working memory, and increase the likelihood of heuristic-driven decisions—shortcuts that may feel efficient but often rely on untested assumptions. A founder who misreads this dynamic may interpret their growing decisiveness under stress as a sign of strength, when in fact it may signal a shrinking capacity for nuanced judgement.

The challenge, then, is not simply to "reduce stress" but to modulate it so that it fuels clarity rather than undermines it. This requires a deliberate approach to pacing decision-making. Consider a founder negotiating a major acquisition under tight timelines. The ambient stress of the situation can create a sense of false urgency that tempts them to gloss over due diligence, rationalising that the big picture "feels right." The disciplined leader recognises that strategic patience—knowing when to pause, gather additional data, or consult contrarian viewpoints—does not weaken their position but strengthens it. In this context, stress becomes a signal to slow down certain processes rather than accelerate all of them.

One of the most effective ways to preserve decision-making clarity under pressure is to pre-commit to process rather than outcome. By defining in advance the criteria for go/no-go decisions, the founder reduces the cognitive load during moments of peak stress. For example, an early-stage founder raising a bridge round might stipulate that they will only accept investors who meet specific strategic alignment criteria, regardless of cheque size. This pre-commitment acts as a guardrail, ensuring that the heightened urgency of dwindling runway does not lead to compromises that undermine long-term positioning. In high-stakes environments, *process discipline is the antidote to stress-driven reactivity.*

Of course, stress management is not solely about mental frameworks. Physiological state and cognitive performance are tightly coupled. Sleep deprivation, nutritional neglect, and physical stagnation—often dismissed as unavoidable sacrifices of leadership—are in fact compounding variables that distort strategic thinking. There is ample research showing that chronic sleep restriction impairs the prefrontal cortex, the brain region critical for executive function, impulse control, and long-term planning. Leaders who treat their physical resilience as optional inevitably degrade their strategic resilience. This is not a matter of "self-care" in the popular sense, but of operational necessity: the body's state directly informs the mind's capacity for high-quality decision-making.

A common counterpoint is that some of the most celebrated business decisions have been made under extreme duress, in conditions where stress was inescapable. This is true, but survivorship bias obscures the fact that for every leader who made a brilliant high-pressure call, many more made catastrophic ones under similar conditions. The difference often lies in how these leaders trained themselves to operate in stressful environments before the critical moment arrived. Military commanders, for instance, conduct extensive simulations that replicate the emotional and cognitive load of battle precisely so that they can act decisively without being cognitively hijacked by stress. Founders, though operating in a different arena, can adopt similar principles—conducting "pressure drills" in the form of scenario planning, pre-mortems, and red-team challenges to familiarise themselves with making consequential decisions while physiologically aroused.

There is also a political dimension to stress as a strategic variable. In post-funding environments, a founder's demeanour under pressure becomes a signal to multiple stakeholders—investors, employees, partners—about the stability and competence of the leadership. A leader who visibly frays under strain risks triggering defensive behaviour in their team and doubts in their investors, both of which can spiral into self-fulfilling prophecies. This does not mean leaders must project unbroken composure at all times, but it does mean they must be conscious of how they metabolise and display stress. The key distinction is between using stress as a driver of constructive urgency versus allowing it to seep into the culture as ambient anxiety.

A useful heuristic for founders is to differentiate between "signal stress" and "noise stress." Signal stress is directly tied to mission-critical issues that demand attention—market shifts, regulatory changes, or major product failures. These are legitimate triggers that warrant strategic adaptation. Noise stress, by contrast, is generated by variables that, while emotionally irritating, have little long-term impact—minor interpersonal conflicts, transient reputational concerns, or low-value operational snags. The ability to separate the two prevents the leadership team from burning cognitive energy on matters that do not alter the company's strategic position. In this way, stress filtering becomes as important as stress management itself.

Finally, there is the question of timing. Not all decisions need to be made in the peak of stress. Effective leaders develop the discipline to create temporal space between stimulus and response. This may mean delaying an investor reply until the next morning rather than answering in the heat of provocation, or restructuring a board meeting agenda so that contentious topics are discussed after rather than before reviewing performance metrics. Such small structural interventions can dramatically reduce the risk of stress-induced cognitive narrowing.

To treat stress as a strategic variable is to reject both extremes: the fantasy of a stress-free leadership environment and the romanticisation of stress as a badge of entrepreneurial toughness. The reality is that stress will always be present in high-stakes leadership—it is the founder's relationship to it that determines whether it sharpens their vision or clouds it. Mastery lies in the discipline to harness stress without being hijacked by it, to let it inform urgency without dictating tempo, and to treat it not as an enemy to be vanquished but as a force to be channelled with precision. In the context of post-funding leadership, where decisions reverberate through complex ecosystems of stakeholders and capital commitments, this capacity is not merely desirable—it is foundational to sustained strategic clarity.

Support Networks That Work: Building peer groups, mentors, and advisors who offer real value

The mythology of entrepreneurship still clings stubbornly to the image of the lone founder, battling obstacles through sheer will and ingenuity. In reality, sustained leadership—especially in the complex, high-stakes environment following a funding round—depends on the quality of the networks that surround the founder. Not all networks are created equal. Some provide tangible strategic value; others become time-consuming distractions or echo chambers that reinforce existing biases. The difference lies in the founder's ability to deliberately construct relationships that act as force multipliers rather than vanity assets. A strong support network is not a large one—it is a precisely engineered ecosystem of people who can challenge assumptions, open doors, and provide informed counsel at the moments when it matters most.

The first critical distinction is between visible support and functional support. A founder might have hundreds of professional acquaintances, regular invitations to industry events, and an impressive roster of LinkedIn connections. None of this guarantees they have people they can call at midnight when facing an existential decision. *True value in a network comes not from breadth but from depth and trust.* It is often the case that a founder's most useful allies are not those who appear prominently in public-facing narratives but those who operate quietly behind the scenes, willing to invest their credibility, connections, or candid feedback without expectation of public recognition.

Mentors occupy a particularly delicate position in this ecosystem. Popular advice frames mentorship as a universally beneficial relationship, but the reality is more complex. Some mentors unintentionally project their own outdated playbooks onto a founder's unique context, offering guidance that feels authoritative but is strategically misaligned. Others may over-identify with the founder's journey, blurring the lines between support and self-interest. The most valuable mentors are those who possess both domain expertise and the humility to adapt their advice to the founder's evolving circumstances. They resist the urge to simply prescribe; instead, they help the founder frame decisions in ways that sharpen strategic thinking. For example, a mentor who has navigated regulatory hurdles in multiple jurisdictions might be less valuable for their specific legal advice—which can be hired—than for their ability to help the founder anticipate the organisational strains that come with prolonged compliance battles.

Advisors add another layer of complexity. While formal advisory boards can be powerful, they can also devolve into ceremonial roles filled for optics rather than impact. Too many founders appoint advisors for name recognition, believing that high-profile associations will automatically translate into credibility and access. While this occasionally works in early fundraising optics, it often fails to deliver practical value when facing operational or strategic dilemmas. A founder should approach advisory roles as if they were recruiting for a mission-critical executive position: with clear expectations, defined engagement terms, and a frank discussion about how success will be measured. Advisors who are unclear about their role, or who are incentivised primarily through equity without active involvement, tend to drift into irrelevance. Conversely, an advisor who commits to quarterly strategic deep-dives, on-call availability for specific issues, and direct introductions into relevant markets can justify their presence many times over.

Peer groups—especially those composed of other founders—offer a different but equally vital form of support. Unlike mentors or advisors, peers are often navigating similar pressures in real time. This creates a unique dynamic: conversations can cut through posturing and focus on the unvarnished realities of leadership. The most effective peer groups maintain a culture of candour and reciprocity, where members share both their failures and their frameworks for decision-making. However, not all peer groups are equally constructive. Some devolve into performative updates where vulnerability is masked by selective storytelling. The utility of a peer group depends on the trust infrastructure: confidentiality must be absolute, and members must commit to offering insight rather than judgement.

A founder building such a network must also recognise the importance of diversity—not in the performative sense, but in the diversity of cognitive perspectives and experience. A network composed entirely of people from the same industry, background, or funding stage is prone to groupthink. Strategic blind spots emerge when everyone in a founder's inner circle draws from similar mental models. Deliberately including people with different sectoral experience, cultural contexts, or even philosophical approaches to business introduces healthy friction. This friction is not always comfortable, but it is precisely what disrupts complacency and prompts more rigorous thinking. A founder deciding whether to pivot product strategy might benefit less from another tech founder's viewpoint than from the perspective of someone who has navigated similar inflection points in a completely different industry.

The practical mechanics of maintaining a high-value network are often overlooked. Relationships do not sustain themselves on goodwill alone—they require intentionality. The founder must allocate time for structured and unstructured interactions, ensuring that contact is not limited to moments of crisis or transactional need. This might mean hosting small, targeted dinners with cross-disciplinary participants, or scheduling regular check-ins that are as much about context-sharing as problem-solving. The most effective leaders treat their networks as living systems: they cultivate them continuously, prune relationships that no longer serve mutual growth, and remain open to integrating new nodes that can bring fresh capability or insight.

Importantly, a high-functioning network also acts as a buffer against the isolation that often follows a funding round. Success can paradoxically increase distance between the founder and their previous circles. Former colleagues or friends may struggle to relate to the new pressures and responsibilities, while investors and board members, however supportive, remain stakeholders with their own agendas. In this transitional space, the right network becomes not just a source of advice but a source of grounding—people who can speak truth without political calculation and remind the founder of priorities beyond the next quarter's metrics.

Yet there is a cautionary note: networks can over-expand, and in doing so, dilute their own effectiveness. An over-networked founder risks spending more time maintaining connections than deploying them strategically. The goal is not to become omnipresent in every industry conversation but to be deeply embedded in a few key circles where influence, trust, and capability align. Each relationship should be justifiable in terms of its potential to sharpen decision-making, expand opportunity, or provide resilience in high-pressure moments.

The real measure of whether a support network is working is not how it looks from the outside, but how it performs in critical inflection points. When a founder faces a major acquisition offer, navigates a public crisis, or decides whether to raise another round, the right network compresses decision timelines, expands the range of considered options, and reduces the emotional toll of isolation. It does not replace the founder's judgement; it fortifies it. In the post-funding phase—when the stakes are higher, the scrutiny sharper, and the margin for error narrower—*a deliberately constructed, well-maintained network is not an accessory to leadership. It is an essential component of it.*

Burnout Prevention: Recognising early warning signs and implementing recovery cycles

Burnout rarely arrives as a dramatic collapse. It is far more often the cumulative outcome of small compromises, deferred rest, and a slow erosion of mental and physical reserves. Founders, particularly in the post-funding stage, are adept at pushing through fatigue, normalising relentless pace as a badge of commitment. This makes them especially vulnerable to missing the early signs. What begins as occasional mental fog during board preparation, or an unusual sense of irritation in otherwise routine conversations, can escalate into sustained cognitive decline, emotional detachment, and impaired strategic judgement. By the time a founder recognises they are operating at diminished capacity, the consequences—missed opportunities, frayed relationships, flawed decisions—may already be in motion.

The most reliable early warning signs are not always the ones people expect. Chronic exhaustion is obvious, but subtle indicators often precede it: a narrowing of perspective in decision-making, where complexity is met with impatience rather than curiosity; a growing resistance to new information that challenges existing assumptions; or an increased reliance on reactive decision patterns instead of deliberate, strategic thinking. Physically, this may manifest as disrupted sleep patterns, fluctuating appetite, or a low-grade but persistent susceptibility to minor illnesses. Psychologically, a sense of emotional flatness—feeling neither excitement in wins nor disappointment in setbacks—can be more alarming than overt distress. *When a founder's capacity to experience proportionate emotional responses is dulled, it signals that their mental system is in protective shutdown.*

Recognising these signals requires structured self-observation rather than ad-hoc reflection. Many leaders assume they will intuitively know when they are burning out, but cognitive biases often mask deterioration until it is severe. Implementing deliberate self-monitoring—such as monthly check-ins against predefined well-being metrics—creates a baseline for detecting deviation. This can be as simple as rating mental clarity, emotional engagement, and physical energy on a fixed scale, combined with feedback from trusted team members or advisors who can observe changes the founder may overlook. The point is not to pathologise every fluctuation but to distinguish between normal cycles of intensity and the onset of chronic strain.

Effective prevention is not about removing stress entirely. For founders, stress is an inherent feature of the role; it sharpens focus in high-stakes environments and fuels bursts of innovation. The problem arises when stress becomes unmodulated—when the system never exits the heightened alert state, preventing recovery. *Burnout prevention hinges on building deliberate recovery cycles into the rhythm of leadership.* Recovery is not simply time away from work; it is active engagement in restorative practices that replenish specific depleted systems—cognitive, emotional, and physiological.

One of the most powerful interventions is micro-recovery: embedding short, frequent resets within the working day. These are not extended breaks or arbitrary pauses, but targeted disruptions to sustained cognitive load—such as stepping outside for a brief walk without devices, switching to a completely different task category for ten minutes, or engaging in deep-breathing exercises that shift the nervous system from sympathetic activation to parasympathetic recovery. Over time, these micro-adjustments reduce baseline stress levels and prevent the slow build-up that leads to burnout.

Equally important is the strategic structuring of macro-recovery cycles. This involves identifying periods—whether quarterly, biannually, or after major strategic milestones—when the founder deliberately exits the operational intensity of the role for an extended interval. The duration and nature of these cycles vary, but the principle is constant: the recovery period must be protected from work-related demands, both in practice and in mindset. Many founders undermine their own recovery by maintaining partial operational involvement, checking investor updates, or responding to "just one urgent thing." True macro-recovery requires a complete psychological detachment from the decision-making sphere, allowing the neural and hormonal systems to recalibrate.

Case examples illustrate the stakes. One technology founder, after an intense eighteen-month product launch cycle, attempted a two-week holiday only to spend most of it troubleshooting remotely. The net effect was negligible, and within six months he faced severe burnout symptoms, eventually requiring a three-month hiatus that disrupted company momentum. Contrast this with another founder who, after recognising irritability and reduced focus as early signs of strain, negotiated with their executive team to delegate decision authority for a month, using the time for both physical rest and structured reflection. The latter not only returned with restored energy but also introduced new operational systems that improved decision distribution, reducing personal load permanently.

Culturally, many founders struggle to embrace recovery cycles because they fear it signals weakness or loss of control to investors and teams. This perception is misguided. Investors and senior teams are far more concerned about the consequences of impaired leadership—poor strategic calls, high executive turnover, missed market timing—than about a leader taking planned recovery periods. Indeed, founders who can articulate their recovery strategy as part of sustainable performance management often strengthen investor confidence by demonstrating foresight and self-governance.

One conceptual shift that can help is viewing recovery not as the absence of work, but as a core component of strategic readiness. Military and elite sports models provide a useful parallel: peak performance is sustained not by constant exertion, but by cycles of intense output followed by deliberate recovery. In these domains, recovery is treated as a tactical discipline—measured, optimised, and embedded into long-term planning. Founders can apply the same principle, aligning recovery with natural business cycles to ensure that critical decisions are made from a position of clarity rather than depletion.

The final dimension is building organisational resilience so that recovery is possible without operational collapse. This requires succession-ready deputies, distributed decision authority, and transparent communication about leadership rhythms. By embedding redundancy and autonomy into the leadership structure, the founder reduces the risk of becoming the single point of failure, which is often the primary barrier to taking restorative time. In well-prepared organisations, the founder's absence during recovery cycles becomes a non-event operationally, and sometimes even a growth opportunity for emerging leaders.

Burnout prevention for founders, then, is less about reacting to crisis and more about engineering an environment where early detection is possible and recovery is non-negotiable. It is a discipline that demands self-awareness, deliberate system design, and the courage to resist the cultural script that equates constant presence with effective leadership. *The leaders who endure are not those who outpace everyone else in the short term, but those who master the rhythm of stress and recovery over the long term.*

Chapter 12
From Funded to Sustainable

The celebration that follows a successful funding round often casts the moment as a company's crowning achievement—a public affirmation that the vision has been validated, investors are convinced, and the path forward is all but assured. Yet beneath the fanfare lies a subtler reality: securing capital is not equivalent to building a durable, self-sustaining enterprise. If anything, it marks the beginning of a more intricate challenge—translating financial inflows into operational resilience and adaptability. History is littered with examples of companies that achieved impressive valuations, only to falter within a few years, undone by fragile business models, reckless capital deployment, or a preoccupation with superficial growth metrics that impressed outsiders while masking underlying weaknesses. By contrast, the companies that endure are those that recalibrate their notion of success once the money is in the bank. For them, progress is measured less by the headline number of the next round than by the organisation's ability to function independently of it.

The first and often most subtle shift is the redefinition of success beyond valuation. In venture capital, valuation operates as both milestone and shorthand for market confidence. Its appeal lies in its simplicity—a single figure signalling prestige, momentum, and competitiveness. Yet valuation, particularly in buoyant markets, is a lagging indicator of sentiment rather than a leading measure of operational strength. True business health is revealed in less glamorous metrics: the stability of gross margins under pressure, customer retention in competitive conditions, the diversity of revenue streams, and the model's elasticity under unexpected shocks. These are the telltale signs of a company capable of weathering turbulence, pivoting without collapse, and preserving strategic independence. Longevity favours those whose operational resilience outpaces their dependence on capital.

Balancing vision with market realities is the second essential discipline. Founders emerge from fundraising emboldened, buoyed by investor belief and capital resources. Yet markets are living systems, often shifting in ways that resist tidy adherence to the original blueprint. The challenge lies in adapting with discernment—adjusting strategy, product focus, or market approach without eroding the foundational purpose that animates the company. This is not compromise in the pejorative sense; it is the careful calibration of principle against pragmatism. Knowing which elements of the vision are immutable and which are tactical allows leaders to maintain coherence while navigating real-world conditions. Confusing the two risks either rigidly pursuing a misaligned model or drifting so far from the founding intent that the organisation loses its identity.

Capital efficiency must become more than a financial target; it must be embedded in the company's cultural DNA. Post-funding environments can foster a perilous illusion: that abundant capital equates to limitless freedom. The temptation to over-hire, over-build, or over-market before the revenue engine can support such scale is ever-present. The most disciplined organisations treat every pound as though it were their last—not from miserliness, but because efficiency preserves optionality. It provides room to manoeuvre in negotiations, resilience during downturns, and leverage when opportunities arise. Crucially, it shapes organisational behaviour: teams begin to evaluate initiatives by impact rather than output, prioritise efforts with compounding returns, and internalise a mindset where measured execution is celebrated. Cultural capital efficiency is not a ceiling on ambition; it is the scaffold that allows ambition to endure through market cycles.

Finally, companies that successfully transition from funded to self-sustaining adopt the long game as their organising principle. This entails resisting the gravitational pull of the next funding milestone as the principal measure of progress, and instead orienting strategy toward self-reliance—where revenues, profitability, and cash flow are sufficient to finance growth on the company's own terms. External capital is not rejected but repositioned as a strategic accelerant rather than a lifeline. The shift requires mental reframing: decisions are judged not merely by their capacity to impress investors over the next year, but by their contribution to the enterprise's viability over the coming decade. This perspective reshapes hiring, product development, market prioritisation, and investor relations—

aligning them with a trajectory designed for longevity rather than perpetual dependency.

The chapter ahead does not advocate slowing ambition; it argues for refining it. Post-funding, the focus must move from short-term validation to enduring capability. The transition to sustainability is neither passive nor inevitable; it demands active discipline, combining strategic patience with operational urgency. The principles explored here challenge the instinct to measure success solely by external signals, offering instead a framework for constructing a business that can thrive independently of market sentiment or capital flows. In doing so, it invites founders and leaders to move beyond the applause of the funding moment and into the quieter, yet far deeper, achievement of genuine independence.

Redefining Success Beyond Valuation: Metrics that reflect resilience, adaptability, and independence

A company's valuation is one of the most visible and least reliable signals of its true health. It is an abstraction—part art, part negotiation, and part market mood—frequently mistaken for an objective measure of value. In early and growth-stage businesses, it is often a reflection of projected potential more than demonstrated performance. The higher the figure, the more intoxicating the narrative. Yet history is saturated with cases where companies celebrated a landmark valuation one year and faced restructuring, forced sale, or collapse the next. The problem lies in the nature of valuation itself: it is not a measure of operational resilience, strategic adaptability, or independence from external capital. It is a snapshot of investor confidence at a given moment, vulnerable to sentiment shifts, sector-wide shocks, and macroeconomic downturns. This means that for founders intent on building enduring enterprises, success must be redefined through metrics that outlast investor optimism.

The first recalibration comes from recognising that *resilience is not an abstract quality—it can be measured.* A resilient business is one that can absorb unexpected shocks without irreversible damage to its operational core. Metrics here include liquidity ratios that ensure the company can cover obligations even during a prolonged revenue dip, the diversity of revenue streams that protect against overdependence on a single market or customer, and operational flexibility that allows cost structures to be adjusted rapidly without gutting capability. Resilience is visible in the ability to continue delivering value to customers under adverse conditions—a reality tested far more rigorously by downturns than by boom cycles. When viewed through this lens, companies that prioritise resilience metrics may appear less aggressive in their growth during bull markets, but they gain something far more valuable: survival during bear markets without having to accept punitive capital terms or strategic compromises.

Adaptability is equally quantifiable, though more difficult to capture in a single metric. It involves the capacity of a business to modify strategy, reconfigure its offering, or reposition in response to market shifts without losing its organisational coherence. Indicators here might include the speed of product development cycles, the proportion of revenue derived from products or services launched in the past two years, or the time taken to execute strategic pivots from decision to deployment. An adaptable business is not one that chases every trend, but one that can interpret market signals accurately and translate them into decisive action. The hallmark of adaptability is not reactive scrambling but structured responsiveness—being able to change direction without dismantling the entire operational framework. Companies that track and deliberately improve adaptability metrics are better positioned to convert market disruptions into opportunities rather than threats.

Independence—the third pillar in this triad—has perhaps the most profound strategic implications. Independence does not mean refusing outside capital; it means retaining the capacity to operate and make key decisions without being hostage to its availability. The most direct measure is the proportion of operational expenditure covered by internally generated cash flow. But it also shows in the optionality of funding decisions: does the company raise its next round because it must to survive, or because it chooses to accelerate? Independence can also be examined through governance structures—whether the leadership has the autonomy to make long-term strategic moves that may not yield immediate returns, without facing existential pressure from the capital structure. In practical terms, independence metrics might include runway length without additional capital, profit margins that allow for reinvestment, and the ability to scale in measured increments rather than in costly leaps dictated by investor timelines.

One of the most instructive examples comes from the contrasting trajectories of two well-known technology companies during the 2000s. Both raised substantial Series B rounds within months of each other, both were lauded for their valuations, and both were pursuing market dominance in rapidly growing sectors. The first, intoxicated by its funding and market narrative, expanded aggressively into multiple geographies, burning through capital at a pace that assumed further raises would be effortless. When investor sentiment shifted following a sector downturn, the company faced a liquidity crisis, was forced into a down round, and ultimately sold for a fraction of its peak valuation. The second company, in contrast, focused on deepening product-market fit in one core geography, refining its unit economics, and diversifying its revenue base before expanding. While its valuation grew more slowly, it reached profitability earlier, retained negotiation leverage in subsequent funding rounds, and weathered the same downturn with minimal operational disruption. The divergence was not a matter of luck; it was the product of fundamentally different metrics of success.

This reframing is not without tension. Many investors, particularly in later-stage rounds, are conditioned to seek rapid valuation growth as the primary indicator of success. Founders who resist this metric as the sole benchmark may face pressure to conform, particularly if peers in the sector are chasing more aggressive targets. Yet the evidence is clear: businesses that anchor their success in resilience, adaptability, and independence not only survive longer but often achieve stronger long-term valuations precisely because they are less beholden to the volatile cycles of capital markets. The challenge is not merely technical—choosing which metrics to track—but cultural, embedding in the organisation a mindset that celebrates these less visible indicators as markers of achievement.

This cultural shift requires disciplined communication. Internally, leadership must make it clear that milestones like reaching sustainable gross margins or reducing dependency on any single revenue stream are as worthy of celebration as closing a funding round. Externally, founders must learn to frame these metrics in ways that resonate with investors and stakeholders, presenting them not as defensive postures but as strategic advantages. For example, a company with a two-year cash runway and profitable unit economics is in a position to reject misaligned investment offers, negotiate better terms, and choose its growth trajectory deliberately—advantages that can be compelling even to valuation-driven investors when articulated well.

The deeper implication is that redefining success beyond valuation changes not only how a business measures itself, but how it behaves. It encourages a posture of long-term stewardship over short-term theatre, of investing in infrastructure that pays off in years rather than in quarters, and of treating capital as a strategic tool rather than as an adrenaline shot. It also builds an organisation's confidence—teams operate differently when they know survival does not hinge on the outcome of the next pitch deck. They take calculated risks, innovate more freely, and engage customers from a position of strength rather than desperation.

Ultimately, the founder who embraces resilience, adaptability, and independence as core metrics is not abandoning ambition but refining it. Valuation remains a useful tool, but it becomes a secondary outcome of a stronger foundation rather than the foundation itself. In an environment where market sentiment can reverse overnight, where sectors can fall in and out of favour in months, and where capital can dry up without warning, these deeper metrics offer something valuation never can: a durable compass for navigating both the highs of expansion and the lows of contraction. The irony is that the companies which deprioritise valuation as their central metric often find that it grows steadily anyway—because they have built something designed not just to be funded, but to endure.

Balancing Vision with Market Reality: Adapting without losing your original sense of purpose

The most enduring companies are rarely those that cling rigidly to their first blueprint, nor those that abandon it entirely at the first sign of resistance. They succeed by walking a narrow and often uncomfortable line—remaining anchored to their founding vision while reshaping their strategies to fit the contours of an evolving market. This tension is not a flaw to be resolved but a permanent state to be mastered. For founders, it is one of the most difficult disciplines to cultivate: the ability to adapt without diluting the essence of what makes the business worth building in the first place. The vision–market balance is so delicate because both forces—steadfast purpose and pragmatic responsiveness—are in constant, sometimes direct, competition for a leader's loyalty.

Vision is the founder's compass. It is the distillation of values, convictions, and ambitions that gives the business its reason for existing beyond mere profitability. It provides coherence to decision-making, a story that inspires teams, customers, and investors alike. But vision alone cannot pay salaries or secure market share. The market reality—the sum of customer needs, competitor moves, technological shifts, and economic conditions—imposes its own non-negotiable terms. A product that fails to meet those terms, no matter how visionary, will fail to survive. The tension becomes acute when the market delivers feedback that runs counter to the founder's original thesis. Do you pivot entirely, risking the erosion of your core identity, or hold firm, risking irrelevance? The answer is neither extreme. The true skill lies in reconciling directional intent with adaptive execution.

History is instructive here. Consider Netflix's transformation from DVD rentals to streaming, and later into original content production. The company's founding vision—to deliver entertainment directly to the customer in a more convenient way—remained constant. But the delivery model evolved dramatically in response to technological infrastructure, consumer habits, and competitive threats. Blockbuster, by contrast, clung to its physical rental model for too long, underestimating the speed at which broadband adoption would change viewing behaviour. Both companies had visions; only one recalibrated it in a way that preserved its core while meeting the demands of a shifting market. The lesson is that vision is not the specific form of your product or service—it is the enduring value proposition that survives format changes.

This distinction is critical because many founders conflate product loyalty with vision loyalty. A market signal that your current offering is underperforming is not necessarily a repudiation of your mission. Instead, it may be an invitation to deliver on that mission in a more relevant, compelling form. The founders who navigate this well tend to maintain a *hierarchy of non-negotiables*: core values and purpose at the top, strategic choices in the middle, and operational tactics at the base. Market changes may force frequent adjustments to the lower tiers, but the upper tiers remain stable. This framework allows for bold pivots without losing the cultural and philosophical backbone of the company.

The opposite mistake—over-adaptation—is equally dangerous. Some founders, in a bid to appease the market or match competitors, end up in a state of strategic drift. They chase every emergent trend, expand into unrelated verticals, or continually rebrand in search of elusive traction. In doing so, they erode the distinctiveness that attracted customers and investors in the first place. Without a clearly defined anchor, the company becomes a mirror of market volatility rather than a shaper of it. This can produce short-term gains but undermines long-term defensibility, leaving the business vulnerable to any competitor with deeper pockets or faster execution.

Maintaining the balance is not a matter of instinct alone; it requires disciplined systems for gathering, interpreting, and acting on market intelligence. The most effective founders institutionalise feedback loops that pull insights from diverse sources—customers, frontline employees, industry data, and strategic partners—while filtering them through the lens of the company's purpose. Not every market signal deserves a response, and not every shift in demand warrants a pivot. The art is in distinguishing transient noise from structural change, and aligning adaptations with the trajectory you are committed to over the long term.

One practical approach is to define in advance the boundaries of acceptable adaptation. For example, a company committed to sustainability might decide it will only pursue growth strategies that reduce, rather than increase, environmental impact—even if market conditions favour a more profitable but less sustainable path. These pre-committed boundaries act as a safeguard against reactive compromises made under pressure. They also serve as a source of credibility in the eyes of stakeholders, demonstrating that adaptability does not equate to opportunism.

There is also a psychological dimension to this balancing act. Founders often form deep emotional attachments to their original product or go-to-market strategy, which can make adaptation feel like betrayal. Conversely, they may overcorrect by seeking market validation at the expense of their original convictions, fearing the risk of irrelevance. Both impulses can cloud decision-making. Effective leaders cultivate a mental model in which the vision is treated as *directional truth*—something that guides and inspires—but not as a set of immutable tactics. This shift in mindset reduces the ego friction that often accompanies change and reframes adaptation as an act of fidelity to purpose, not a departure from it.

Examples from outside the technology sector reinforce this point. In consumer goods, Patagonia has consistently adapted its product lines, retail strategies, and marketing channels to meet changing customer preferences and global trends. Yet its vision—to produce high-quality gear while advocating for environmental stewardship—has remained unwavering. This coherence between purpose and adaptation has strengthened its brand equity and allowed it to weather competitive pressures without resorting to tactics that dilute its identity.

The real test of balancing vision with market reality comes during periods of sustained external pressure—economic downturns, disruptive innovations, or sudden regulatory changes. In such moments, the temptation to deviate from core purpose in the name of survival can be overwhelming. Here, the founder's role is to act as a translator between the immutable and the mutable: to articulate how the company's purpose remains relevant in the new context, and to redesign strategy so that purpose is not only preserved but made more salient by the adaptation. This reframing can rally teams, reassure investors, and signal to the market that the company is both grounded and responsive.

Ultimately, the companies that master this balance operate with a dual awareness: they are vigilant observers of market forces yet deliberate custodians of their original intent. They adapt not because the market dictates it, but because adaptation serves the deeper mission. This discipline protects against both the rigidity that leads to obsolescence and the shapelessness that erodes identity. For founders, it is less about finding a fixed equilibrium and more about developing the capacity to navigate the shifting point between the two forces, again and again, without losing the plot. In doing so, they create organisations capable of both evolving with the times and outlasting them.

Capital Efficiency as a Cultural Value: Embedding financial discipline into the DNA of the company

The ability to raise capital is often mistaken for the ability to use it wisely. In the early stages of a company's life—particularly in a climate of abundant funding—there is a tendency for financial discipline to take a back seat to rapid expansion. Resources flow easily, burn rates climb, and the assumption takes hold that the next round of funding will arrive before the current one runs dry. This mindset can become dangerously embedded in a company's culture, eroding the very qualities that would make it self-sustaining. *Capital efficiency is not merely a financial metric; it is a cultural choice that shapes the behaviour, priorities, and resilience of an organisation.* When it becomes part of a company's DNA, decision-making shifts from "Can we afford this now?" to "Does this investment create lasting value relative to its cost?"—a far more demanding and clarifying question.

Capital efficiency is often misunderstood as synonymous with frugality. While both involve managing costs, frugality is reactive and narrow, focused on limiting outlay. True capital efficiency is strategic: it is about achieving the maximum possible return on every unit of capital deployed, whether in marketing, product development, hiring, or infrastructure. It involves the continuous optimisation of resource allocation to drive long-term enterprise value, not just short-term profitability. In this sense, capital efficiency is as much about where and how you spend as it is about how much you spend. A company can burn through hundreds of millions and still be capital efficient if those investments compound into defensible market advantages—just as a company spending modestly can be capital inefficient if those resources are misallocated or fail to generate durable impact.

Cultural adoption of capital efficiency begins at the top. The founder's own relationship with money becomes the template for the organisation. Leaders who view capital as a scarce, high-cost resource—even when their accounts are flush—tend to foster sharper decision-making across the company. This mindset is not about instilling fear of spending, but about instilling respect for the fact that every pound or dollar invested represents equity dilution, risk assumption, or debt burden. By framing capital as *time bought*—time to prove the business model, win customers, or develop the next product—the leadership keeps the organisation anchored in the reality that capital is a finite strategic asset, not a safety net.

The structural challenge lies in embedding this principle into everyday operations. This is where culture becomes the decisive factor. An organisation's financial habits are not shaped solely by the finance team; they emerge from the accumulated choices of managers and employees at every level. If a sales team believes that overspending on customer acquisition will be tolerated because revenue targets matter more than margins, capital efficiency collapses. If engineering prioritises elegance over delivery speed without weighing the opportunity cost, the same erosion occurs. A culture of capital efficiency creates an environment where these trade-offs are openly discussed, quantified, and resolved in line with both financial and strategic goals.

The most disciplined companies operationalise this culture by creating transparency around the cost–benefit calculus of major decisions. This means not only tracking metrics like CAC (Customer Acquisition Cost) or payback periods, but making them visible and understood throughout the organisation. When employees can see how their actions influence capital deployment and capital recovery, financial discipline ceases to be a finance-department concern and becomes a shared responsibility. This visibility is particularly important in venture-backed companies, where the sheer scale of available funding can dull the perceived urgency of resource constraints.

A common pitfall is treating capital efficiency as a periodic consideration rather than a constant one. Some companies only become conscious of efficiency when fundraising becomes difficult or when investors demand improved unit economics. By that point, cultural habits may be too entrenched to shift quickly, and the company faces a painful period of forced austerity. The stronger approach is to embed efficiency from the outset, even when funding is plentiful. Doing so builds a muscle memory for disciplined spending, making the organisation more resilient in downturns and more deliberate in upturns. It also serves as a form of signalling to investors and partners, demonstrating that growth is being pursued on sound, sustainable terms rather than on a cash-fuelled gamble.

There is, however, a nuanced tension between capital efficiency and speed. In highly competitive markets, moving fast often requires heavy investment—sometimes ahead of revenue or before efficiency is demonstrable. The challenge for leadership is to distinguish between necessary, calculated over-investment and undisciplined spending. Amazon's early years are a classic example of the former: the company operated at a loss for years, not because of inefficiency, but because its capital was deliberately deployed to build infrastructure and market dominance that would yield massive long-term returns. The difference lay in the rigour of its decision-making and the clarity of its ultimate strategic intent.

The cultural embedding of capital efficiency is reinforced by aligning incentives with long-term value creation rather than short-term activity metrics. Compensation structures that reward revenue growth without regard to profitability invite capital waste. Conversely, tying bonuses or equity vesting to efficiency-linked metrics—such as lifetime value to customer acquisition cost ratio—encourages teams to think in terms of sustainable performance. In practice, this can mean rebalancing the scorecard so that operational and financial discipline carry equal weight with top-line growth.

Symbolic acts from leadership can be equally powerful in shaping cultural norms. When founders publicly scrutinise their own spending decisions, travel economy instead of business class, or decline unnecessary perks, they send a signal that restraint and rigour are valued. These signals often have more influence than formal policy, because they demonstrate that capital efficiency is not an abstract principle but a lived behaviour. In contrast, leadership hypocrisy—preaching discipline while indulging in extravagance—can undermine years of careful cultural cultivation in a matter of weeks.

Case studies reveal that capital-efficient cultures tend to share a few common traits: they institutionalise regular post-mortems on failed projects to extract lessons about resource misallocation; they encourage cross-functional collaboration to ensure that strategic priorities drive spending; and they avoid "vanity spend"—investments made primarily for optics rather than substance. These behaviours, once normalised, create a reinforcing loop: capital efficiency leads to better decision-making, which leads to stronger performance, which reduces reliance on external funding, which in turn strengthens the company's bargaining position with investors and partners.

Ultimately, embedding capital efficiency into the company's DNA is not about being conservative; it is about being deliberate. It is a philosophy that resists both reckless expansion and paralysing caution. When fully realised, it empowers a company to grow on its own terms, maintain independence of action, and weather the inevitable fluctuations of the funding environment. In a landscape where capital can appear limitless one year and scarce the next, those qualities are not merely advantageous—they are existential.

The Long Game: Thinking beyond the next round to a self-sustaining enterprise

For too many founders, the horizon is defined not by the health or independence of the business, but by the next funding milestone. Pitch decks, investor updates, and strategic planning sessions revolve around runway and valuations rather than durability and autonomy. Yet the companies that endure—the ones that grow into self-determining enterprises—are those that master the discipline of looking beyond the immediate influx of capital. *The real game is not about securing the next cheque; it is about building an organism that can thrive without one.*

A self-sustaining enterprise is not a romantic ideal. It is a pragmatic objective grounded in the reality that capital markets shift, investor sentiment cools, and competitive advantage is fleeting. Even the most promising venture can be undermined by an over-reliance on external funding. The moment the capital pipeline narrows, the enterprise's entire strategy is tested. In contrast, a company structured for long-term sustainability can choose when, whether, and on what terms to raise capital. This freedom is not just financial—it is strategic leverage. It allows the founder to negotiate without desperation, to reject misaligned investors, and to avoid making existential compromises for short-term liquidity.

Thinking in decades rather than rounds forces a redefinition of success. Instead of measuring progress solely in terms of valuation, headcount growth, or geographic expansion, long-game companies track the quality and durability of their cash flows, the strength of their customer relationships, and their operational adaptability. The venture-backed ecosystem often treats profitability as a distant milestone, but founders playing the long game integrate profitability into their early mental models—not necessarily as an immediate target, but as a clear eventuality. Profitability is not just a financial outcome; it is a marker of control, the point at which the business sustains itself without external subsidy.

This shift in perspective also reorients decision-making about growth. Hypergrowth strategies often assume that market dominance achieved today will convert into defensible profitability tomorrow. But dominance is fragile when achieved at unsustainable cost. Playing the long game requires balancing growth ambitions with an understanding of their capital implications. It means asking whether each incremental customer is worth the acquisition spend, whether product expansion is diluting focus, and whether operational complexity is outpacing the company's ability to manage it effectively. Scaling is not abandoned—it is paced and shaped to serve resilience, not vanity.

Companies that embody the long game tend to cultivate a conservative approach to core operations while maintaining calculated boldness in innovation. This duality is crucial: an organisation cannot survive indefinitely by simply protecting what it has, nor can it thrive by recklessly chasing every new opportunity. Apple, for example, invests heavily in R&D and product differentiation, yet runs one of the most disciplined supply chains in the world. That operational precision gives it the stability to take creative risks without jeopardising its fundamental health. For founders, the lesson is clear: sustainability is rarely achieved through uniform caution or relentless aggression—it emerges from an intelligent interplay between the two.

One of the more difficult aspects of adopting a long-game mindset is resisting the gravitational pull of investor expectations. Investors often operate on fund timelines that prioritise liquidity events within seven to ten years. Their return horizons may not perfectly align with the founder's vision for an enduring business. Navigating this tension requires exceptional clarity about whose goals are being served by each strategic choice. Some of the most sustainable companies in history have been built by founders willing to trade short-term investor enthusiasm for longer-term autonomy—deliberately avoiding overcapitalisation in order to maintain strategic freedom.

Cash flow discipline becomes the operational expression of this philosophy. While a round of funding may temporarily mask inefficiencies, long-game founders view every expense through the lens of future self-sufficiency. This does not mean starving the business of essential investment; it means ensuring that capital is consistently directed towards assets, capabilities, and systems that will continue to generate value long after the latest funding has been spent. In practical terms, that might mean prioritising investments in customer retention over speculative marketing, or in process automation over office prestige.

Importantly, thinking beyond the next round also demands resilience planning. Economic cycles, regulatory changes, and competitive shocks are inevitable over the lifespan of an enduring business. Founders who have internalised the long-game mindset build in buffers—financial reserves, diversified revenue streams, adaptable supply chains—so that the business can navigate turbulence without scrambling for emergency capital. This resilience does not appear overnight; it is the cumulative result of consistent, disciplined decision-making over years.

There is a psychological dimension to all of this. The adrenaline of startup life often comes from big, binary events—product launches, funding announcements, headline partnerships. But the long game is sustained by a quieter satisfaction: watching operational metrics improve, seeing customer lifetime value rise steadily, observing the compounding benefits of strategic patience. This requires a temperament that can tolerate deferred gratification, that can view each round of funding as a tool rather than a trophy, and that can accept the slower, more deliberate pace of building something meant to last.

Counterintuitively, companies built for self-sufficiency often find it easier to raise capital when they choose to. Investors value predictability and control as much as they value growth potential. A founder who can demonstrate that their business could survive without the cheque they are asking for is, paradoxically, more likely to get it on favourable terms. This flips the usual dynamic: instead of investors determining the founder's options, the founder determines the investor's relevance.

Ultimately, the long game is a philosophical commitment expressed through operational discipline. It acknowledges that while external capital can be an accelerant, it is not a business model. Founders who embrace this view build enterprises that remain viable through market cycles, leadership transitions, and shifts in capital availability. They view funding rounds not as lifelines, but as strategic tools deployed on their terms, in service of a business designed to endure long after the cheque clears.

About the Author

Avery Stanton has spent years inside venture-backed companies, moving from early operating roles to advising founders once the term sheet is signed. Stanton's work centers on the messy, high-stakes stretch between funding and sustainable scale—where governance, numbers, and narrative have to align. A frequent facilitator of founder roundtables and board-ready planning sessions, Stanton develops practical frameworks for capital deployment, milestone design, and investor communication. The writing is shaped by a simple conviction: money speeds everything up—including mistakes—so disciplined stewardship is a founder's real edge. Avery contributes essays on scale-up leadership and hosts small, off-the-record salons for founders wrestling with post-funding decisions. When not working with teams, Stanton refines decision tools that help leaders pace growth without losing control of their companies—or themselves.

www.ingramcontent.com/pod-product-compliance
Lightning Source LLC
Chambersburg PA
CBHW031346230926
51848CB00002B/402
9789371770477